Flower Arranging
for Special Occasions

Pamela Westland

Photographs by
Nelson Hargreaves

Columbus Books
London

Frontispiece: romantic, soft colours for a
very special occasion such as a wedding
or christening party, featuring heavily
scented stocks, ranunculus and carnations.

Copyright © 1985 Pamela Westland

First published in Great Britain in 1985 by
Columbus Books
Devonshire House, 29 Elmfield Road, Bromley, Kent BR1 1LT

Westland, Pamela
    Flower arranging for special occasions.
    1. Flower arrangement
    I. Title   JJ. Hargreaves, Nelson
    745.92′6   SB449.48

Designed by Pat Craddock

Typeset by
Goodfellow & Egan Ltd, Cambridge

Printed and bound by
New Interlitho Milan

ISBN 0 86287 182 4

CONTENTS

INTRODUCTION

If you have ever rushed out into the garden to cut a few flowers just before guests are due to arrive, or bought a bunch of flowers on impulse at a stall on the way home, you have made – already, in that one act – a statement. The colours you decide to put together, the flowers you choose – modest violets, prolific weeds or great, showy, eye-catching blooms – the container you select, be it an old teapot or a gypsy basket, and the way you cut and arrange the stems all contribute to the finished effect, and reveal as much about your mood, likes and dislikes as does your handwriting.

Give half-a-dozen people a bunch of daffodils, a couple of sprays of foliage and an old pickle jar and you will be presented with half-a-dozen different arrangements. One person might think you cannot improve on nature and plonk the stems in just the way they are; another might cut them to graduating heights so that each flower is seen to best advantage; one might strive for a symmetrical outline and another favour a lopsided look. They will all have perfectly good reasons for their choice, and they will all be 'right'. For surely the only valid aim when choosing and arranging flowers is to create a design that is pleasing to you.

I go along with the old adage that 'every picture tells a story', and certainly hope that every photograph in this book does at least that. With each arrangement, whether it expresses the most casual of moods or celebrates a special occasion, I have tried to convey my own feeling for flowers; which is, in a nutshell, that I like them to look as natural as possible and, most of all, to have a friendly, cottage-garden kind of look.

Because arranging flowers *is* such a personal pastime, we decided to take most of the photographs (all, in fact, except those in a church) at my home. Our old Essex farmhouse took very kindly to being turned into a photographic studio, with lights, tripods and reflectors, jugs, pots, vases, trays, trugs and baskets of flowers all over the house, barn and garden.

Behind the scenes

However casually you like to arrange flowers, there is no skimping the preparatory work. In most cases the arrangement itself is only the tip of the iceberg. The care you take in harvesting the flowers at the right stage and even at the most suitable time of day, the way you help them acclimatize to the shock of being severed from the plant ('conditioning'), and the situation you eventually give them in the home all have an effect on their healthy good looks and their ability to give lasting pleasure.

As a general rule, all flowers should be cut just before they are fully opened (and certainly before they have played host to bees) and at a coolish time of day. If you cut the flowers in the full heat of the noon-day sun when they are already gasping for drink, they may never fully recover. Stand the stems straight in water – yes, it really does mean taking a bucket round the garden – and if at all possible leave them in water in a cool, dark place overnight. Re-cut the stems with the secateur blades and the stems under water before you arrange them.

When you buy flowers give them the best possible chance of fulfilling their promise by giving them a long, cool drink and re-cutting the stems as described.

Among the various plant types there are a number of special cases which need to be treated in a particular way. Woody stems, for example, need a little help in taking up water freely by scraping and splitting or crushing the stem ends, and those with sappy stems, like poppy and all the spurges, need to be singed over a flame to seal the ends.

You will find this kind of instruction in full, besides many helpful hints and tips (such as not standing an arrangement in a hot, sunny window), facing the colour photographs to which they refer. The index will help you to locate this information quickly.

Out of sight

The text describes everything you need to know about how the artless arrangements in each photograph were carefully contrived. For as all flower-arranging enthusiasts soon learn, even the designs that appear most 'easy' and 'natural' have been achieved with the aid of a little hidden subterfuge. Without blocks of stem-holding foam, pieces of crumpled wire netting or a handful of marbles, many of the most casual designs would look too casual by half!

I hope that 'old hands' to the art will bear with me, as they go through the book, when I explain to beginners what effects these materials (sometimes called mechanics) can help to achieve: with a raised block of soaked foam, for example, stems can be positioned to slope downwards, almost vertically – of great advantage in any tall container – and with the aid of wire netting you can angle stems just the way you want them in the widest-necked of containers.

Rising to the occasion

Probably, like me, you try to have a few flowers around the home at any given time. But most of us make a special effort when we are expecting visitors. Flowers are by far the nicest way to show guests how welcome they are.

For that reason, the book not only follows through a complete year of flower-arranging, from the first few precious buds of springtime to the last bright berries of winter. It is divided into sections, each one dealing with an occasion or a special cause for celebration, and I hope that in each group you will find designs to spark off your own imagination and give you further ideas.

If you are giving a party, there is a design to suit every mood – a few geranium heads in a pottery dish for an impromptu occasion (you do have to take your courage in both hands and cut all the stems short), a basket of poppies for a country-style effect, and a couple of more elegant presentations, illustrating the first steps in using stem-holding foam.

The emergence of spring, in the flower-arranger's eyes, really is something to celebrate. Designs here show how to focus attention on the minimum of flowers at a time when they are scarce and how to go to town with armfuls of bulbs when the market is awash with them.

Three sections are concerned with different ways of sharing the countryside or your garden with friends. Weekend guests are made to feel at home with a zingy pot of poppies, a meadow-sweet jar of delicate wild flowers and a romantic cherub holding aloft a nosegay of scented blooms. To take when you go visiting there is a pot of herbs – pretty yet practical – and two highly portable posies. And to open your garden in fine style, there are *al fresco* designs coupled with tips about choosing colours that glow at twilight, containers that will not tip over, and striking colour combinations.

No matter how practised one is at arranging flowers, it is on occasions that really matter – weddings, christenings, anniversaries, special birthday parties or harvest thanksgiving at the church – that one is apt to get a nasty attack of cold feet. No need! The designs in these sections show, I hope, that you can achieve extra-pretty results by following your usual scheme of things. The designs can have the same informal appeal, the same spontaneity; some of them are merely bigger.

The very word 'pedestal' has been known to strike terror in the heart of many an experienced flower-arranger. But tall designs, raised on a stand so that they can be seen clearly from a distance, need not be at all complicated. The closest any design in the book comes to being 'formal' is the English pedestal arrangement on page 43, for which there is extra guidance.

The flower-arranger's year ends, in December, with a celebration as in times past of holly and ivy, hips and berries, candles and ribbon bows – the coming together of vibrant evergreens and rosy fruits, the presentation of traditional designs from the heart, the satisfaction that, bedecked, our homes are looking their best.

There may be times throughout the year when you want to capture the beauty of the flowers, seedheads and leaves in the hedgerows and gardens. The section called Lasting Mementoes and the notes on pages 86–8 tell you how to preserve plant material by air drying, powder drying, in a glycerine solution and by a process descriptively termed skeletonizing. With a stock of preserved materials carefully stored away, you can create designs to invoke the best of the seasons' colours, at any time of year.

Welcome, as you go through this book, to Spices, the setting for my favourite ways to present flowers. I hope some of them will become your favourites.

Pamela Westland

GIVING A PARTY

A gleaming white stand brimming over with headily-scented carnations; a craftsman-made basket tumbling with a sheaf of straight-from-the-cornfield flowers; glinting glass and spattering, flickering candles on a polished table; chunky pottery a blaze of glory with brilliant scarlet geraniums – the flowers we choose and the way we arrange them can set the scene and accurately capture the mood of occasions of all kinds.

As entertaining is becoming more casual and carefree, flower designs are following suit. A great cornucopia spilling over with the most expensive blooms the florist can supply would look wildly out of place on a table set for spaghetti, and would hit a visually jarring note. Nowadays, where flowers are concerned, the natural look is beautiful. A pot of poppies might look so simple that it just 'happened'; but those poppies need to be picked at their best, carefully handled (more of that later) and treated with consideration – which usually means keeping them away from direct sunlight, heat or strong light.

When it is a question of setting the scene for a dinner or buffet party the container should complement the pottery or china being used for the meal. An ideal choice could be a piece of the tableware not actually being pressed into service, perhaps a spare sauceboat, cream jug, shallow dish or cup and saucer from a matching tea-set. Otherwise, choose something with the same 'feel' – plain white pottery or porcelain to partner a patterned set, or a piece picking up one of the colours of the china pattern.

Here is the perfect way to give a new lease of life to a favourite piece that has met with an accident. An unsightly chip or missing chunk can be completely concealed behind a trailing leaf or carefully placed flower. If the container is cracked and no longer watertight, you can line it with an inner container, perhaps a foil baking dish, to hold the water, or fit it with a piece of wet stem-holding foam.

The arrangement's height will depend upon the table setting. A flower design that is to be placed between guests seated round a table should be discreetly low. Craning necks do not make for a ready flow of conversation, and intrusive arrangements will not inspire compliments. For a buffet table, on the other hand, the design should be raised well above the level of the food so that it can be seen from a distance. If the occasion is a stand-up drinks affair, when all the tables and other surfaces will be viewed from above, make sure that this is the most flattering angle for your flowers. A geometric shape such as a posy ring could be the prettiest and most practical choice.

A blaze of geraniums

Someone has arrived unexpectedly for a meal and you need flowers for the table? No problem. Some of the most stunning designs are ones you can do in a trice with no special equipment.

The container in the photograph opposite was a pottery butter dish – with a chipped rim. Chunky, speckled and in the same greeny-grey neutral colour as the tableware, it has a fresh lease of life as a vase.

The geraniums were picked on a quick dash to the garden or greenhouse, but chosen carefully, nevertheless, so that they are not *all* in that lovely zingy bright red. Notice how a few pale salmon pinks and deep cyclamen blooms actually draw attention to the purity of the red. Without them the reds would become an almost indistinguishable blob.

As the container is shallow with a wide neck, the stems must be cut really short. Taking scissors to perfectly long, straight stems and ruthlessly chopping them off just below the bloom can be as unnerving as cutting into a piece of expensive silk to make a dress. But it has to be done. Then the flower heads will stay put, forming a hummocky cushion.

What other flowers would give similar results? A mass of mixed zinnias, including some of the beautiful Persian Carpet variety in pink, red, orange and yellow, or pom-pom dahlias, perhaps in red, orange and coral, would be very striking. A mixture of different colours of phlox, some pale pink ones distributed among deep mauve, cerise and purple would be unusual (another example of a long-stemmed flower type which, once cut down, makes an eye-catching cluster). Or you could use a couple of spray chrysanthemums, or sweet peas in strong colours, rather than pastels.

For an informal occasion: a rectangular dish filled with a mass of short-stemmed red and pale pink geraniums.

ALL POINTS OF VIEW

The curtains are drawn, the lamps lit and the table is set for a small dinner-party. The focus of attention, from before the first course until the end of the meal, is the flower arrangement in the centre of the table.

For this sort of occasion it is often worth opting for a design with a fairly well-defined shape such as a triangle or an almost-triangle, which in floral art circles is known as an asymmetrical triangle.

You can form this kind of design on practically any shape of container. For a really low-lying effect you can use a flat dish or plate – maybe one from the dinner service. Items with natural pedestals, such as cake stands, take perfectly to the shape, too, with tendrils of leaves trailing prettily over the rim. Or you can create the illusion of a pedestal with other house-hold items – a sturdy wine- or brandy-glass on a stem, an upright, straight-sided sauceboat or even, as in the photograph opposite, an egg stand.

A flower design raised slightly above the table top is both elegant and eye-catching. But be sure that it does not reach face level and get in the guests' way.

A block of water-holding foam raised above the rim of the container provides the flowers with the necessary nourishment and gives you scope to direct the stems at will. You can buy the almost weightless green foam in florists in two sizes, in small, sturdy cylinders and in large rectangular blocks, to use whole for large designs or cut up to any required size. You can also buy inexpensive light plastic 'saucers' in white or green, purpose-made to hold the cylinders. They have retaining rings in the base, just the right size to hold them firmly. Or you can improvise by using the upturned lid of a coffee jar or similar lid.

Soak the foam in a bowl of water for 20–30 minutes until it is thoroughly saturated and feels heavy. It is then ready to use, and should be kept topped up with water to keep it permanently moist. Without a saucer you can wedge the foam directly into the neck of a container, but in some cases this makes topping up a messy procedure and can lead to water marks on furniture. The foam can be used over and over again until it disintegrates, but you cannot re-soak it; so store it, still damp, in a sealed plastic bag.

Whenever you use 'mechanics', hidden supports for the flower stems, they must be firmly attached to the container. Many a beautiful design has come to grief through lack of care at this stage. Stick the plastic saucer to the container rim with a few dabs of Plasticine or the florist's equivalent, OasisFix, which stays in place no matter how wet it becomes. Or use special florist's green tape, again almost impervious to water, taping over the foam and round to stick it firmly to the container. Or use old-fashioned twine to tie round and round like a parcel. The heavier the flower, the more care is needed with this preparation.

A flower arrangement for a table centre must, like a piece of beautiful embroidery, have no 'wrong' side. For double-sided displays it can be a good idea to divide the flowers into two more or less equal groups so that you do not complete one side of your masterpiece only to find yourself left with a couple of wilting wallflowers for the other. Take out the flowers to be seen from all points of view, the central one and side trails, then divide up the others equally.

The double yolker

The egg-cup stand featured opposite has been turned into a mini pedestal by the use of a white plastic saucer and a cylinder of soaked foam. That way the freesias can be placed horizontally and with a downward slope and some of the leaves hang almost vertically to conceal the holding materials.

Brilliant red flowers can be too stark a contrast against a gleaming white holder. Here the border carnations, creamy white fringed with coral red, bridge the gap between these two extremes. The freesias, trumpet-shaped and perfect for side points, repeat the soft flame colour and the tiny zinnias are rich red.

Place the topmost flower and the side points first. Then make a fan shape of mixed foliage on each side of the arrangement to cover the stems and mechanics. Cut short the carnation and zinnia stems and place the flowers first on one side and then, turning the arrangement round, the other. The long trails of herb robert, both stems and leaves turned autumnal red, echo the colour of the zinnias.

A double eggcup does double duty as a mini pedestal for
a triangular arrangement of carnations, zinnias and freesias.

KEEPING IT CASUAL

It is a light, bright summer's night, the invitation said 'Come as you are' and the food is set out buffet-style in a country kitchen. Here is a chance to make a really breathtaking flower arrangement that is so casual it looks as if it grew that way.

To make a bold and lasting impression, go for flowers which really spar with each other in shape and colour. Vivid clashes that might jar in the close proximity of a dinner-table can stand their ground without difficulty at a buffet. Huge, voluptuous scarlet peonies teamed with yellow tree lupins; multi-coloured ranunculus with sea-blue perennial cornflowers; huge white cabbage roses with flame-coloured gaillardia – all these would be cheerfully unforgettable.

Taking the basket

For containers with an appropriately home-spun and rustic look, you cannot beat baskets. They are perfect at all times and everywhere. From a tiny posy basket crammed with a child's first offering to a deep fruit basket spilling over with pineapples and passion flowers, they somehow always look right. Yet, beautiful though they are, baskets never steal the limelight from the flowers.

Luckily it is the easiest thing in the world to build up a varied collection very cheaply – as long as you have space enough to store them. And if space is at a premium, turn the baskets into a decorative feature while they are waiting to become practical: hang shopping baskets, clothes baskets and trugs from the kitchen ceiling, and sticky-tack plate- and dish-shaped ones to a garden-room wall.

At first sight cane and rush baskets might seem anything but practical as flower containers. For a start, they do not hold water. But there are ways of making them work, so do not be put off by improbable shapes as you do the rounds of the ethnic shops, charity sales, market stalls and department stores. Look out, too, for wooden items you can pick up for a song – or even free. Those large round boxes used for Brie, for example, make excellent flower trays and can usually be yours for the asking.

To use deep, bowl-shaped baskets for flowers, stand a water-holding container such as a baking dish or tin inside, or – depending on the design you have in mind – push in a piece of soaked florist's foam. To build an arrangement on a flat basket, tray or board, you can fix a container that will be rendered out of sight, out of mind by large leaf forms. Use a saucer with a cylinder of foam, or a piece of foam wrapped in foil – a wise precaution to protect polished wood surfaces.

Cutlery hold-all

A bleached cane cutlery basket can serve a dual purpose. At the beginning of the party this one was filled with up-to-the-minute red-handled knives, forks and spoons. Now it's just a pretty face.

The holding material, wedged into one side of the horizontal compartment, is a piece cut from a block of florist's foam and wrapped almost to the top in foil.

The flowers and plant material have been chosen for that wandering-through-the-cornfields look. The bright red poppies with their flat, velvety faces and deep black centres are blended with one of the largest of the wayside flowers, huge pure white marguerites. Because one flower is dominant for its piercing colour and the other wins on points for its sun-ray shape, each complements the other. The daisy shape, always irresistibly pretty, is echoed in miniature form with wild chamomile and garden feverfew.

Green oats, which look as if they are still gently swaying in the breeze, further emphasize the cornfields theme. The variegated leaves, picking up the colour of the wall background and linking it with the oats, are periwinkle. These leaves benefit from, and poppies positively need, special pre-arranging treatment – singeing. *See page 26* for details.

Begin the design by placing the tallest and the longest stems, the oats which rise right out of the picture and extend beyond the basket at both sides. Push them firmly deep into the foam to keep them rigid. Next position the poppies that form the triangular outline, then the large marguerites and the poppies that fill the centre. Close the gaps with the tiny daisy flowers, short stems of oats and the periwinkle leaves.

Poppies, most vivid and eye-catching of flowers, strike a gloriously casual note in a cutlery basket for a country-style party.

ALL THAT GLISTERS

A highly polished table, glistening glass, candles and delicate lace-like flowers – you can tell there is a party in the offing. A tall, slender design on a narrow container looks graceful in the centre of a buffet table. It is tall enough to catch admiring glances from a distance and, being head and shoulders above the food, is perfectly practical. It takes up minimal space on the table so plates can be crowded all around and underneath it.

There are masses of possibilities for tall, narrow containers of this kind. The one opposite is a no-money-back wine carafe, perfectly proportioned for flowers because it is wide at the base – a point worth considering for a help-yourself party. Other candidates could be large glass storage jars, completely at ease in a kitchen or country-style party setting, large cosmetic jars – some of them are highly decorative – and old ginger-beer bottles.

The glory of glass lies in the fact that it glitters. So wash all glass containers thoroughly and polish them with a relish. Any stubborn marks inside can be removed by swishing raw rice grains about in warm water and detergent.

If you want to add a spot of colour without sacrificing the twinkle you can fill a glass container with coloured water. Just a few drops of food colouring, ink or cold-water dye can bring the holder into colour line with your table setting and the flowers. And of course you can ring the changes time and again.

To achieve this 'Long Tall Sally' effect with other containers, you can create a design a-top pottery or brass candlesticks, using a special holder, decorative tube-like biscuit tins or even tall, narrow vases, setting the flowers *on* rather than in them.

Airy-fairy flowers

For these up-in-the-air designs choice of flowers is all-important. Large blooms such as chrysanthemums and some dahlias would not only look top-heavy, they might actually prove to be so.

Flowers which habitually grow beside water look specially good with glass, and lilies of all kinds seem to be ideal. For a look of luxury, try teaming two colours of dainty, speckled alstromeria, perhaps the pale lemon and the peach, with in-fillers of smaller flowers in deeper shades. It will look luxurious, but it will not be expensive – two sprays will be enough.

In spring, you might choose dainty white jonquils with cream double narcissus and a few grape hyacinths for colour accent and shape variety, and in winter you could hardly do better than a small handful of Christmas roses with some trailing pale green hellebores: those with red-etched edges look specially festive.

Whatever the flowers, you will need a few flattish leaves at the base to cluster round and conceal the holding material, and some long trails to snake down well below the container rim. If, by mischance, the design had a more or less horizontal cut-off point it would look distinctly ill at ease.

Structuring step-by-step

In the design on the facing page, the stems are held in a cylinder of foam fixed into a purpose-made plastic saucer. Use florist's clay, tape or twine to attach it to the carafe. If you use a candlestick instead, you can make it ready for its floral role by using a special 'candle cup', a more deeply dished saucer that holds the foam and is formed with a wide plug on the base. This fits into the candle aperture and gives you the beginnings of a firm grip, but you will still need extra fixing material.

Position the tallest stems first. Those in the photograph are fennel seedheads, a delicate yellowy-green, and the dainty white umbrellas of cow parsley. With the stems pushed close beside each other into the foam, arrange them in graduated heights, the tallest at the back and each one in front of it progressively shorter.

Then make a cushion of the concealing leaves, in this case lime green cupressus, followed by the stems fanning out at the sides – more fennel.

Now position the 'real' flowers, cream spider chrysanthemums and buds, with the largest blooms – stems cut short – closest to the centre and the buds tailing off at the sides. Add wisps of frondy leaves – asparagus or maidenhair fern would be just as pretty as the fennel.

When space is at a premium on a buffet-table,
a tall container is the answer.
This glass wine carafe is ideal for lending
extra height to spider chrysanthemums.

13

FULL CIRCLE

A circlet of flowers is one of the prettiest of decorations, reminiscent of the flower hoops carried on long poles by Spanish and Portuguese children in procession at carnival time. It owes something to the enchanting headdresses worn by children for May-day festivities, and by tiny bridesmaids in attendance at summer weddings.

This type of design is destined to be viewed from above, by guests standing in groups at a drinks party, perhaps, or toasting the bride in a garden marquee. So it is especially important to check that it passes this bird's-eye view with flying colours.

The magic circle

The base, which makes working the design child's play, is a green plastic hoop about 25 cm (10 inches) in diameter. You can buy these from florists. You fill the channel with small off-cuts of green foam and then set about covering them completely with flowers and leaves.

An alternative is to improvise by using a large biscuit tin lid or, better, a wooden Brie box or lid. Make a circle around the rim with small foam blocks. Using a wooden base, wrap the underside of the foam in foil to avoid seepage. Fit the blocks close together, but do not worry about the gaps. Large flowers like marguerites and flat leaves, such as ivy, will bridge them competently.

Soak the foam thoroughly before launching on the design. When it is dismantled, store the whole contraption in a polythene bag ready for another occasion. The circlet can be completely transformed with holly and candles for Christmas (*see page 85*).

The ideal flowers

As all the flower stems have to be cut short and pushed close against the foam this is a perfect way to use leftovers from other arrangements. All the small side shoots, broken stems, untidy snippings and insignificant buds are brought together in a table-top design that would perfectly match a pedestal or, indeed, the bridal bouquet.

Choose a mixed colour theme for the strongest impact – pink, white and blue; orange, cream and violet; pink, green and purple – and select flowers with an interesting variety of shapes, just as you would for a larger, more conventional arrangement.

You will need some large, flat-faced flowers for the focal points; to use only small wispy ones will not be effective. Gardens and market barrows are full of suitable options – purest pink mallow, glowing golden eschsholzia, deep purple pansies (you would need to poke holes in the foam first, to help the slender stems penetrate), the whole spectrum of anemones, russety rudbeckia and so on.

Smaller flowers in toning colours make pretty links in the flower chain – as do the daisy-like feverfew and wild chamomile in the photograph opposite: they are the single white chrysanthemums in miniature.

Some full, round and solid flowers stand out well in the crowd. Roses and rosebuds are perfect. Completely different examples, to tone with your colour theme, could be double tagetes, pom-pom dahlias, double spray narcissus or cushion-topped and frilled carnations.

Trumpet shapes give the circlet an 'open' look. As well as alstromeria, our choice, you could have separate foxglove flowers (remember you do not *need* much stem), aquilegia, nerines, lilies and the tube-shaped varieties of narcissus.

Then there are the all-important fillers, tiny snippings you can push in to fill the gaps – dainty lime green alchemilla mollis and spotty, snowflaky gypsophila in our example. Heathers, astilbe, forget-me-not and limonium are other possibles.

Lastly, you will want a handful of leaves, preferably ones with a clearly defined outline. Shiny evergreens like ivy, spotted laurel, magnolia and eleagnus all catch the light and send back shafts of brilliance. Avoid dark matt-surfaced leaves, which only absorb light, and tender young deciduous leaves, because these are notorious for wilting.

Pretty as a bridesmaid's headdress and practical for a low coffee table, a circlet of summer flowers is one of the simplest designs to make.

THE JOYS OF SPRING

Spring flowers come upon us with a suddenness that is amazing. One day it seems there are nothing but evergreens in the garden, and the next there are several clumps of perky little flowers heralding the glory to come. One day the flower markets seem to have nothing but all-the-year-round flowers grown in greenhouses, for which over-familiarity can breed at least boredom, if not contempt. And the next there are boxes and boxes of the specialities of spring: the sunshaft colours of narcissi, daffodils and tulips. From a few early blossomings to abundance in a matter of days, the change is dramatic. Those are the two extremes captured in the designs in this section, from a wispy handful of the first garden flowers, to the subsequent glorious profusion.

All kinds of narcissi, including daffodils, have soft, sappy, fleshy stems that do not take well to being pushed into foam. To give them the best chance of a long life indoors, stand them in water and hold the stems if necessary by other means.

Underwater activity

When you cut narcissi from the garden it is specially important to adhere to the golden rule for *all* flower-gathering – take a bucket of water with you and dunk the cut stems in it immediately. It might seem strange at first to be going round the garden with a bucket instead of a trug, but your arrangements will benefit in terms of life-span. If you are buying your flowers, cut about 2.5 cm (1 inch) off the bottom of the stems, holding them under water, as soon as you get them home. When the stems are cut a seal is made naturally over what is in effect a wound. Cutting the stems below the water line – in a washing-up bowl, for instance – prevents an air lock from forming. Air locks prevent the stems taking up water and keeping fresh.

Follow the same practice again when you need to cut the flowers to the required height as you arrange them. It is a counsel of perfection for all flower stems, but pays the highest dividends with the fleshy ones.

Before you arrange them, leave the stems almost up to the flower necks in a bucket of cool, but not icy cold water for several hours if possible, in a cool, dark place. Think of it as rehabilitation – a pause for refreshment after the shock of severance. This is an important step in what the floral art world terms 'conditioning'.

Planned nonchalance

For some reason, there is a strong compulsion among would-be flower-arrangers to dump a bunch of daffodils unceremoniously into a straight-sided vase, and leave it at that. The design opposite, a collection of yellow spring flowers silhouetted against the stark February sky, is a compromise around that theme. The container, a green-glazed cooking pot, has an aperture far too wide to hold the stems without support. So a piece of crumpled wire netting – chicken wire, which you can buy by the metre or yard – is wedged into the top, domed slightly above the rim and rammed securely against the sides.

The netting has 5-cm (2-inch) holes, but when the wire is firmly crushed between the hands, these are reduced considerably. The network of holes, irregular now in size and shape, gives you the means of arranging stems that will stay upright in even the widest containers.

The flowers span the yellow palette from the palest cream of the double-cluster narcissi through the deep gold of the tulips to the contrastingly sharp orange centres. Deep green ivy leaves merge into the container colour and variegated periwinkle punctuate the yellows. The greyish-green tulip leaves, erect at the back of the design, strengthen the outline.

Stems are not usually the most beautiful part of a plant, and those of spring flowers are no exception. Graduating the flower heights, so that those in front conceal the stems behind them, takes care of the problem. Some of the flowers at the very front of the design rest on the rim and others are angled to hang slightly below. To do this in a wire-and-water combination, push the stem diagonally backwards, angled towards the centre of the container.

No matter how sullen the sky or how stark the trees, a pot of lemon-yellow narcissi is a beautiful and reassuring harbinger of spring.

A PRECIOUS FEW

When it comes to spring flowers, there is no doubt that small is beautiful. The blazing yellows and reds of narcissi, daffodils and tulips are magnificent, but it is the modesty of the tiny clumps of primroses, violets, snowdrops and celandines that captures our hearts.

Exquisite as these flowers are individually, they are most attractively displayed in small bunches, either slightly rag-tail as when a child has picked them, or made up into small, neat, Victorian-style posies. Casual or contrived, it is the tight-little-dome effect that is so appealing.

Children, with a natural instinct for the fitness of things, choose the simplest of containers for their tiny offerings – preserve jars, especially decorative six- or eight-sided ones, enamel mugs, pottery beakers – all of which are ideal.

These delicate stems are not suitable for arranging in foam but, though it might seem absurd to mention 'holding materials' at all in the context of such informal wildings, crumpled chicken wire can be useful, especially if you want to use a deep or wide container. Just a small piece of wire about 11.5 cm (5 inches) square squashed into the neck of a beaker or small bowl enables you to cluster the flower heads prettily.

In the window

For the spring flower study opposite – no one would call it an arrangement – the choice of container is deliberately low-key. The beaker, banded with muted green, blue and brown, has a matt surface which puts all the emphasis on the flowers. Although no flowers should be placed in strong light or heat, the pale shafts of spring sunlight slanting through the window are a positive advantage, especially for dark-coloured subjects such as violets or pulmonaria.

Among the earliest flowers to appear in the garden, blue, mauve and pink pulmonaria are a perfect foil for the pale yellow of primroses and – if you can beat the birds to them – golden primula. You might know pulmonaria by their other, regional and affectionate names – such as lords and ladies, soldiers and sailors, and lady's hatbands.

The pulmonaria stems are placed criss-cross first in the beaker, making a natural network to hold the tender primula stalks, and the two colour groups are almost completely separated – just a few mauve and blue flowers creep in among their paler neighbours to form a link.

Victorian posies

A delightful and charmingly traditional way to arrange primroses, violets and other small flowers is in tiny posies – like the ones the gypsies used to sell.

To make a circular posy, arrange a fan shape of leaves – primrose leaves with primroses, perhaps shiny and not-too-dark ivy leaves with violets – in one hand. Arrange the flowers against the leaves, coaxing them into a gentle, round curve rising towards the centre. Bind the stems with fine twine and trim them level.

These little nosegays can then be displayed in a variety of ways. Stand one in a wine-glass for each place at the dinner-table, or in a scent bottle on a dressing-table. Put an inner liner in a flat basket, stretch a piece of chicken wire across the top, and place a few bunches close together, side by side, making a cushion of flowers.

Nostalgic and delightful, these little posies make the most welcome of gifts. There is no nicer way to share with someone the joys of spring.

The first few flowers of the season – pulmonaria and primula – are among the most precious of all, seen to best advantage in small, contrasting posies.

A SPLASH OF COLOUR

Take a bunch of tulips; take your pick from the shrub blossom burgeoning in the gardens; close your eyes and choose almost any container from the cupboard and you have the makings of a striking still-life group.

For tulips are nothing if not arresting. Buy them from the flower barrows and you can have any colour you like, as long as it is plain red, yellow or white. Buy them from a florist and you have the choice of far more subtle tones. My favourites, far and away above all other tulips, are the palest shade of apricot, which look fabulous with deep sienna and burnt orange wallflowers.

Grow tulips in your garden, patio and windowbox and you hardly know where to begin – still less where to finish. Now you can plant ahead for the day when you can team Maja, a deep golden flower that looks as if someone with a great deal of patience has snipped minutely all around the petal edges, with winter jasmine and shiny and matt evergreens in a green container.

For a majestic – some might think somewhat sombre – effect, you can marry the deep mauve of Blue Pearl with spiky grape hyacinths, adding plenty of blue-grey leaves – ballota, maybe – for good measure.

More romantic arrangements could feature Angeligne, the pearl-pink tulips shaded with pale green, and hellebores – a neat combination of shade and shape – or Princess Irene, picking up the mauve flashes on these pale coral tulips with clutches of heather.

A pot of tulips

Our choice of deep red tulips edged with white meant that a white china container was in order. Without the touches of white in and around the flower petals, it might have been too overpowering.

The neck of the teapot is fitted with crumpled wire netting. First the stems of the flowering currant (having already been treated: *see page 58*) are arranged, to establish height and width. Then come the tulips, but not before they, too, have been pre-conditioned (see below).

The tulips are graded for height, the stems of the tallest ones barely noticeable against the green wall that almost matches them. And, as they get shorter, they are angled so that the flowers face outwards, revealing the pattern of the stamens against the white centres. Amusingly, the fully-opened Ribes flowers are like the tulip centres in miniature.

Keeping them straight

Everyone who has ever arranged tulips knows how awkward they can be. You stand them upright in a container, turn round, and they have flopped down like rag dolls, as if all the life had gone out of them.

To prevent this happening, you can do two things. As soon as you have cut them, or get them home, re-cut the stems under water (*see page 16*). Wrap the whole length of the stems closely around with several thicknesses of newspaper or stiff card to just below the flower heads. Stand the stems deep in a bucket of cool water and leave them in a cool place for several hours, or overnight.

Before arranging the tulips prick through each stem just below the head with a darning needle or pin. This releases any trapped air. And, as always, keep the container topped up with cool, clear water.

Teapots of all kinds make particularly pretty flower containers and are worth seeking out in junk-shops and market stalls.

DUTCH INFLUENCE

Whether we cut spring flowers from the garden or buy them on joyous impulse from a street market, there are plenty of reasons to be grateful to the Dutch bulb-breeders. For it is in Holland's research laboratories, testing stations and bulb farms that gradual improvements are made possible in vigour, strength, form, shape, disease-resistance and colour, which is still the average gardener's main consideration. Every year those of us who 'grow our own' take for granted that the spring bulb catalogues will have something new to offer – and every year they do. Perhaps it may be a dwarf form of an old favourite; tulips with frilled, cut or spiky petals; novelty colours such as palest pink or icy green in double tulips, or, as in recent years, these exquisite new colours in daffodils, too.

These innovations would not be possible without the complicated and lengthy breeding programmes undertaken by the horticultural and agricultural scientists, cross-breeding (to put it at its simplest) a bulb which has, say, a popular colour combination with one which is valued for its stability.

Commercial growers responsible for offering us the best possible cut flowers for the longest possible period look mainly to Holland for the steady improvements in the bulbs they buy under licence to grow in their own fields. One of the most arresting of agricultural sights, these giant patchworks of red, yellow, cream, white and orange are not, in fact, a display of flowers destined for our vases. Each patch, a field-strip of perhaps several acres, is planted with bulbs strengthening up in their second year, before they are mature enough to cut, the following year, for market.

Then they will be harvested at what daffodil growers call the 'green pencil' stage, when the flower colour is barely visible at the tip of the enclosing calyces but will slowly emerge in transit. That way the growers will have done their best to see that the flowers we buy are as fresh as can be and in tip-top condition. The rest is up to us. *See page 16* for how to treat daffodils, in particular, and *page 20* for tulip care.

A way with colour

The Dutch influence can rarely be far away when a bowl of narcissi, daffodils and tulips is being arranged, for it is almost impossible to be unaware of the beautiful flower compositions of the Dutch and Flemish Old Masters. These artists showed us how to group even the three primary colours, red, yellow and blue, in a charming and sympathetic way.

The large display opposite of spring flowers in mixed colours could take the centre of a stage for a public meeting or prize-giving, give visual warmth to a fireplace not in use or, standing four-square on the floor, brighten an empty corner or entrance porch.

The container is a pottery casserole fitted at the neck with crumpled chicken wire. Because of the volume of flowers used, the wire is not only firmly wedged into the aperture, but for extra security tied with twine to the handles.

In a group of mixed colours, one is almost always dominant. In this case it is the red; though often, in a blend of muted tones, white will be pre-eminent. This strongest colour should not usually be used at random, but in a positive way, in a flowing arc, an echelon, straight line or cluster, to avoid a spotty look.

The fan-shape is outlined by placing the yellow irises first. Then the thick band of red tulips is brought strongly through the centre. Single and double white and cream narcissi and yellow and white trumpet daffodils are cut to graded heights to fill the shape, with a few tulips – most of which are partially concealed behind other flowers – at the sides.

A mixed bag of foliage – tulip, cupressus, ivy, young hazelnut and forsythia – provides colour weight around the base of the design, and lightweight fingers of green at the edges. And, for the final touch of spring, there are sprays of dried mimosa, no longer rivalling the bulb flowers for hyper-brilliance, but still heady with that unmistakable polleny perfume.

With two of the primary colours, red and yellow, predominating in the selection of flowers, the third one, blue, is the strongest possible contrast for the background.

For a hallway, the corner of a room, or to fill an empty fireplace, a huge bowl of spring bulbs – narcissi, tulips and irises – makes a cheery and colourful impact.

EASTER MORNING

Coming down to an egg for breakfast on Easter Sunday morning is all the more enjoyable if it is filled with flowers! Eggshells are among the prettiest of miniature containers for tiny posies, and they rank high with children who find that kind of decoration, simple as it is, exciting and memorable.

Luckily traditional cooking for Easter, after the long Lenten fast, calls for quantities of eggs. Save them up for a week or two beforehand.

Break each egg close to the top, the narrow end, and tip out the egg. Wash the shells in warm, soapy water and turn them upside-down to dry. Deep brown eggshells are hard to beat for colour and texture. But for a brighter splash you can aerosol-spray them with matt or gloss paint – the ends of cans of car enamel can be used up in this way.

To do this, invert each broken eggshell over a piece of dowel or a pencil and spray it evenly with paint. Leave to dry and then, for a touch of magic, splatter it with short, sharp bursts of a contrasting or toning colour. Or comb the wet paint instantly for a rippled effect; spray two colours and wipe them with a tissue pad for a marbled effect. You can even spray through stencilled shapes.

Your eggshell colour choice will depend on the flowers available. Strong, bright blue looks good with pale primrose yellow, deep violet and all the soft pinks. Dark 'racing' green is striking, too, especially with a white theme of snowdrops and daisies; you will need pale lime green or yellow foliage snippings such as cupressus or golden privet for an effective colour contrast.

How do you use your eggshell vases? It will come as no surprise to find that they look pretty in egg-holders of all kinds: primroses, primula, daisies and deadnettles for a chunky pottery carrier; an even daintier medley of micro flowers – purple and white violets, early sprigs of aubretia, speedwell and forget-me-not – for eggshells gracing a Victorian piece; and a bigger and bolder selection for a wooden egg-holder in the kitchen. Grape hyacinths, periwinkle, celandine and trailing miniature ivy would be in keeping.

Separate little containers give you a chance to flatter everyone (or anyone lucky enough to have an early-morning tea-tray) with an arrangement of their own. At any other season a mini posy sits prettily in an eggcup, small preserve or spice jar or, according to the time of day, shining bright wine or jigger glass. At Eastertime, the posy goes in the eggshell which goes in the container, and it looks more festive.

For the centrepiece for a children's party paint-sprayed eggshells can sit in mix-and-match sprayed cardboard egg-boxes. Bright yellow boxes, blue eggs and zingy yellow flowers – or the complete reverse – keep to the traditional Easter colours and have child appeal. Six flower-filled eggs in six spaces would be over the top. Leave some recesses empty, graced perhaps by trailing leaves; or fill them with whole sprayed eggshells, a handful of marbles, glass baubles or tiny fluffy chicks.

Flowers under the microscope

It is quite a challenge in March or April to go round the garden on a floral treasure-hunt and pure delight to discover one or two heads of this, a tender tendril of that. Violets and primroses are naturals and they are our choice, an obvious one, for the container in the foreground (opposite). One deeply-veined ivy leaf polished till it shines not only complements the tiny flowers but helps to make the most of a few.

The eggshells in the pottery holder carry two linking colour themes. On the left, violets, yellow-centred primula and blushing lawn daisies nestle in a circle of ivy leaves. On the right, the mauve is taken up by brilliant, velvety primula and a few cineraria.

No garden to comb? Then take snippings from house plants and buds from sprays of florists' flowers. Longish trails of miniscule mind-your-own-business foliage and tiny variegated ivy, scented pelargonium leaves and frondy maidenhair fern provide the greenery. You can buy primroses and violets and add small buds from sprays of freesia or single chrysanthemums for a slight change of scale.

For good measure – after all, it is Easter – there is a posy of violets and ivy leaves decorating the straw hat. See how to make a posy on *page 18*.

If plenty of broken eggshells are left over from the Easter cooking, what could be prettier to hold dainty clusters of primroses and violets?

WEEKEND GUESTS

A splash of brilliant colour on the breakfast-table, brighter than any early-morning TV show; a tumble of stoic flowers for a pleasant surprise when the bathroom door is opened; an arrangement thoughtfully designed to match the curtains or a picture on the spare-room wall, a posy on a tea-tray – there is nothing that more clearly tells guests they are welcome.

Having people to stay gives you the excuse, should you need one, to fill your home with flowers. For guests who are staying reach rooms that other guests might not reach. With all the other advance preparations necessary, this is not the time for ambitious arrangements. Match the flowers meticulously to your colour schemes and the atmosphere your home creates, and keep the designs simple.

First things first. Flowers in the hall give guests an immediate lift when they arrive after a journey. But there are halls and halls, and some make the very idea of a container spilling over with flowers laughable. Or do they? Even the narrowest passage or landing has space on the wall for a vase. If your sympathies are with the *art nouveau* or *art deco* eras, or you follow the fashions of the 'forties and 'fifties, you could spend some happy hours combing antique and junk shops for pastel-coloured, shell-shaped, moulded-plaster relics. For something more contemporary, patronize craft shops and markets for hand-made pottery or basketware wall-vases.

Prepare for the flowers by filling the neck of the container with a sticking-up wedge of soaked florist's foam partly wrapped, in the case of a basket holder, in foil or polythene. Then your flower design can be an expansive cornucopia of mixed blooms or perhaps, for the hand-crafted containers, a cluster of contrasting foliage types with just a few bold flowers as accents.

Guests doing a stint in the kitchen will find the task less arduous – so will you – if there is a fresh and pretty arrangement or a pot of herbs among the pots and pans. The one on *page 37* gets the ratio of effort (minimum) to effect about right. It also incorporates scented leaves to pinch in passing.

For the bathroom, apt to suffer periodically from steam heat, choose good-tempered flowers known to last well. There are not very many wild ones in this category, but all umbrella-shaped flowers such as yarrow and cow parsley survive almost indefinitely, go with anything and, with their soft mistiness, could not be less clinical-looking. Marguerites, most charming of daisies, deadnettles, spurge, broom and everlasting pea are other 'hardy' wildings.

Among garden and florists' flowers it is the casual ones that look most at home on the bathroom window-sill or cosmetic shelf. A pot of marigolds, zinnias or tagetes lets the floral golden sun shine in, flowers in the pink range – be they asters, pinks, columbine or michaelmas daisies – bring a warm glow to a whitish scheme and will still be standing long after you have waved the guests goodbye.

Popular poppies

Fresh as the early-morning dew, a creamy-white vase of brilliant red poppies matching the tableware is really worth getting up for. It will last for the weekend and way beyond if you treat the stems properly (see below). Then arrange them casually, as naturally as they grow. To be different, push in a few stems of deep blue larkspur, to echo the dark poppy centres.

Singeing stems

Any stems that 'weep' a milky fluid, such as poppies and euphorbia, should be sealed by burning. Otherwise the fluid eventually solidifies, sealing over the stem ends and preventing them taking up enough drinking water.

To keep the flowers fresh for as long as possible, cut the stems and hold them in a candle, match or gas flame until they turn black. Stand the stems in tepid water; if you need to shorten them for your arrangement, singe them again.

Tender leaves which wilt quickly – periwinkle, for example – also benefit from singeing.

Burning the stem ends need not be quite as time-consuming as it sounds. You can singe more than one stem at a time in a single flame, and when you have a large number to treat you can work up a quick and steady rhythm by holding two stems in each hand in two side-by-side candle flames.

Like all flowers with milky stems, poppies
need special treatment if they are to look
fresh and bright and last well in water.

MEADOW-SWEET

Buttercups and daisies, campion and cow parsley, woodruff and willowherb: wild flowers have a natural charm that can never be matched by their more showy hybridized and cultivated cousins. That makes them the perfect choice for a bedroom arrangement to greet city-dwellers and gardenless guests.

Do not forget that the picking of many wild flower species is forbidden. Check which species (broadly, the most common plants and rampant weeds) are on the permitted list before you put scissor to stem.

Wild and wonderful

Whether you gather flowers in the wild or grow them in the garden, they provide inspiration for some delightfully simple flower arrangements – even with weeds. Among the tiniest, a jug of snowy-white mouse-ear chickweed with trails of sky-blue periwinkle and the minute mauve flowers of ground ivy would be a pretty early-morning offering on a breakfast tray. Or team purple and white clover flowers with silvery-white fumitory and snippings of valerian.

As the ratio of leaves to flowers is on the high side in most wildings – which breeders spend a lifetime attempting to reverse – it is a good idea to strip off all or some of the leaves. Deadnettles, for example, do not look so impressive with their hoops of tiny flowers under a canopy of dull, all-enveloping leaves. But strip off the foliage and you reveal white, yellow, pink or mauve flowers quite as pretty as wild orchids; unlike orchids, they are on the 'free' list for picking. Comfrey, bugle, mallow and ground ivy also benefit from leaf-pruning.

Many of the wayside umbrella flowers make the prettiest of decorations. A large shopping basket of white cow parsley speckled with red campion would fill a summer fireplace to perfection; a pot of frothy sheep's parsley veiling a few pink gerberas or carnations makes a romantic wedding arrangement, and yarrow, that hardiest of umbellifers, blends well with, say, white marguerites and sprays of butter-yellow broom.

Flowers picked in the countryside need to be carefully prepared for the journey home. Try to pick them in the coolest part of the day, the morning or evening, and as close as possible to the time you leave for home.

Strip off all the lower leaves and wrap the stems in wads of damp tissues or, for tiny flowers, balls of cotton wool. It is a good idea to put small ones into a polythene bag and tie the top so that they reside in a permanently moist atmosphere. Then keep them as much as possible in the shade – in the boot of the car rather than on the back window ledge. As soon as you get the flowers home give them a good long drink in tepid water. If you do not need to arrange them straight away leave them in a cool room overnight.

First aid

However much care you take with flowers, some will wilt. To revive them, re-cut the stems under water, then either float the flowers for a few minutes in a bowl of water or, if, like composites, they are reasonably substantial, dunk them in head-first. Then stand them in water again for as long as possible. Flowers and foliage with woody stems can usually be revived after re-cutting by being stood for a minute or two in boiling water (wrap tissues or paper round flower heads to protect them from the steam).

Flower picture

The oil painting of a summery meadow inspired the design of wild flowers on the facing page.

In this group, the plant materials are in an 'adjacent colour' theme: yellow and green are next to each other on the colour wheel, and in the rainbow. The scheme is based on the sharp, lemony green of the spurge.

The container is an earthenware mustard pot fitted with a plastic saucer holder and a cylinder of soaked foam (*see page 8*). The foliage close against the foam is placed first, to give, as it were, adequate ground cover. Next comes a froth of sheep's parsley, to give a full-circle effect. The spurge, with its stems pre-singed, are placed so that the largest ones form the focal point close to the centre base, with smaller examples extending to the sides. Pale yellow deadnettle and brilliant white campion are eye-catching features. Last but not least are the twisty, twirly stems of buttercups, some with flowers still in bud and others sporting the domed centres exposed when the petals have dropped.

The painting of a summer meadow inspired this simple arrangement of country flowers – spurge, sheep's parsley, deadnettle, campion and buttercups.

A HINT OF PERFUME

It is a lovely idea to pamper your guests by choosing lightly scented flowers and leaves for an arrangement in their room, so that even on the dullest of days they can bask in the scents of summer. However, it is wise never to choose hyacinths – some people find that extra-heady perfume unacceptable. Something infinitely more subtle is called for.

A pot-pourri of garden and wild flowers makes a dainty arrangement in a cherub vase. Our choice *opposite* is a blend of scented garden pinks and wayside campion, with the stabilizing influence at the base of variegated ivy. Other lovely combinations would be sweet peas speckled with gypsophila, and tendrils of clematis trailing over the container. A single bunch of freesias works wonders, scent-wise, and is pretty teamed with a cluster of toning anemones, and lamonium or periwinkle trails to link flowers and holder. And in the spring, grape hyacinths and primroses could be borne on a scented tide of lily-of-the-valley.

Roses are most people's favourite flowers, and there can be few who do not marvel at the scent of the old-fashioned kinds. A bowl of heavenly-scented pink and yellow musk or damask roses with pale apricot antirrhinums gives an easy-on-the-eye blend of 'rounds and points'. If your choice is the delightfully wayward pink and white unscented dog roses from the hedgerows, you can import perfume with a sprig or two of jasmine or a handful of clove pinks, the 'gillyflowers' of Victorian times.

Short-cut stems of Brompton stocks in pink, cyclamen and white make a colourful straight-from-the-garden display on their own, or you can use a few of the long stems as the 'points' to scent an arrangement with, say, straggly two-coloured pelargonium or trumpet-shaped petunias. Wild lupins that grow in profusion along sandy seashores are another richly-perfumed flower spike. Team these pale lemon-coloured flowers with, for example, white roses and a couple of blue lace-cap hydrangeas or, less formally, with drooping branches of gold or cream viburnum opulus.

Sprigs of lavender have quite enough perfume and more to 'carry' anything you care to put with them. To avoid a spiky look, tie several heads together into a bunch and use them, clustered, instead of full, round flowerheads. That way they team well with pink and cream late-season tulips or delicate white single Japanese anemones and lime-green alchemilla mollis by the handful – always indispensable as a filler.

If you have growing herbs or other aromatic leaves on the windowsill, or better still a choice in the garden, these can provide scent for flower arrangements of all kinds. A few scented pelargonium (commonly called geranium) leaves decoratively tucked among the flowers are inviting to the touch – you pinch them to release a waft of lemon, orange, cinnamon, nutmeg, rose and other fragrances. Lemon balm, mint and marjoram, especially the golden variety, are among the best soft-leaved herbs to mingle with flowers. Fennel is fabulously frondy and rosemary retains its pungency even once it has dried.

Angel delight

The pretty pink and white arrangement opposite would make any guest feel instantly at home. The green cherub container extends to a cup-shaped holder at the top, and a piece of soaked foam is strapped in with florist's tape. When the arrangement is dismantled wash the container, top up the foam with water and tie a polythene bag round to enclose it. Then it will be ready for use again.

The variegated ivy leaves are placed first, at the base and the back, where they avoid a spotty, see-through effect. Stems of pinks in white and three shades of pink are short-cut so that some of them nestle close against the foam and others trail outwards at the sides. Sprays of pink and white campion and white mouse-ear chickweed are used as fillers with short sprays of sheep's parsley putting the finishing touches.

Variegated ivy leaves, without looking too heavy, make a pretty frame for the spray pinks and dainty wildings – campion, sheep's parsley and mouse-ear chickweed.

THE PERFECT GIFT

Whatever the sentiment you wish to convey – 'thank you for asking me' as you arrive for a meal or a party; 'thank you for coming' to a visiting VIP; 'happy birthday' or 'get well soon' – flowers are the perfect gift. And whatever the circumstances, they will be all the more appreciated if they are presented in a container, or ready to pop in a vase without fuss.

The container can be part of the gift, the memento that lasts when the flowers are just a memory. Light, easy to carry when you go visiting, and unbreakable, baskets are ideal. A gypsy basket of primroses and violets, a miniature trug with a pot of primulas and a foam-held cluster of narcissi and freesias or a wall decoration with a difference, a shoulder shopping-basket spilling over with traily honeysuckle and roses: these are just a few possibilities.

Practical and pretty pottery and china also make good containers to keep. A single cup and saucer is transformed into a precious gift, for Mother's Day perhaps, with a nosegay of rosebuds or ranunculus inside; an earth-brown pottery beaker looks positively zingy filled with buttercups and daisies; and a medley of sweet-smelling herbs would be especially appreciated by someone who is ill at home or in hospital.

To present to a visiting celebrity, or to someone who opens a fête, gives the prizes at a speech day or draws the raffle at a charity event, a sheaf of flowers is ideal. It is, after all, the thought that counts, and a spray of garden flowers and foliage can be just as lovely – and often more imaginative – than an expensive offering in cellophane and ribbon from a florist's.

No garden to gather from? If the spray is for a formal presentation, buy, say, a few long-stemmed carnations, a trio of alstromeria sprays, a bunch of anemones and some eucalyptus foliage and assemble them in your own style. For a more personal touch, you can achieve the cottage-garden look with the most inexpensive of flowers such as long-stemmed single chrysanthemums, tight round heads of sweet william and cornflowers backed by a fan of fern leaves.

Colour coding

When you make up your own floral gift, the colour scheme is entirely in your own hands. If it is someone you know well, it is a pretty compliment to colour-code a spray to match the recipient's living-room or bedroom colour scheme, or to devise an arrangement in her favourite colour. Otherwise, play safe and opt for palish colours that will not clash with anything, no matter what she is wearing. Pale apricot, deep cream and yellowy greens; soft pink, powdery grey-blue and deep greyish greens; white, cream and brightish greens would all be good choices.

The daisy spray

Fresh as a daisy, the casual spray opposite takes only moments to assemble and, with its backing of variegated, scented lemon balm leaves, is specially suitable for someone who has no garden or is house-bound.

Make sure the spray gives lasting pleasure by taking special care with the preparation. You will want to use tender young foliage for the clearest, sharpest colours; but then it is at the most vulnerable stage. Put the stems in water as soon as you cut them. Singe them in a candle flame (*see page 26*) or dip them in boiling water for a few moments, then give them a good, long drink of water.

Marguerites are among the most good-tempered of flowers and a happy choice for a presentation. Pick them several hours or the night before and stand them deep in water.

To make up the spray, arrange an elongated fan-shape of foliage flat on the table. Then place the flowers in graded lengths on top, the line broken up by a band of short-stemmed leaves. In the picture, the gaps are filled in with alchemilla mollis. Gypsophila, pearl everlasting or feverfew, all clusters of tiny white flowers, would be other options.

Bind the stems close to the lower flowers, then bind on a small posy or other special feature just above the grip. A pretty choice in our green and white design would have been a circlet of lawn daisies ringed with more lemon balm leaves. For simplicity, and in step with the aromatic theme, we chose instead a full, round cluster of bright green angelica seedheads.

See page 34 for more detailed instructions on assembling a flower sheaf.

Marguerites, among the most sturdy of garden and wild flowers, are good travellers and the ideal choice for a simple but elegant posy to take as a gift.

SUMMER GARDEN

Here is a flower sheaf to present with pride, as evocative as a stroll round a cottage garden, as romantic as a Victorian valentine, and as practical as it needs to be to survive happily until the end of a lengthy social occasion. This design would be perfect for a child, or adult, to present at a special function.

There are certain guidelines to follow for all presentation flowers. First of all, the spray must be comfortable to hold, for both the giver and the receiver, which means that it must be well-balanced and never top-heavy. If a young child is making the presentation, scale the arrangement accordingly. There could be many a slip 'twixt platform and step if the child cannot actually see over the foliage.

Then there is the question of neatness. As with all flower arrangements, the back of a spray must be attractively finished. A few flowers tucked in among the backing foliage will give the design all-round interest and lighten the whole effect. Without them the flowers may look, when glimpsed from the 'wrong' angle, for all the world as if they have been glued to a piece of green card.

A feel for foliage

The foliage serves a number of purposes. For one, it provides a firm foundation for flowers of all shapes and sizes. For another, it frames the flowers attractively, like a well-chosen mount around a picture, and shows them off to their best advantage. Most of all, the leaves protect the flowers on their way to and from the event, as they are handed over and handled; it is the foliage that takes the raps.

Choice of foliage is of the greatest importance. Do not fall into the trap of playing safe with dark green ivy, laurel, camellia or rhododendron. Evergreens do get high marks for strength and durability but plain dark leaves score badly for interest, strongly resembling that lack-lustre cardboard backing just mentioned.

Pale silvery green eucalyptus is attractive. Spotted laurel is good if the flower selection is fairly positive, but no good at all if the blooms are small and speckly too. Deeply-cut fern leaves are guaranteed not to look heavy, and lime green cupressus mixed with other foliage, hebe for example, can be effective. It goes without saying that stems with thorns are out. If you do choose rose leaves or, indeed, stems of roses, meticulously strip off every last thorn.

Mixed foliage gives a delightfully informal look. For the design opposite, angelica, fennel, yarrow, marjoram and poppy leaves were collected in a bucket of water. Treated carefully (*see page 32*), these all last well.

There are no right and wrong flowers for a sheaf. More important is the balance of colour, shape, size and texture. You can colour-grade the flowers from dark at the handle to pale at the top – perhaps a posy of marigolds close to the grip, yellow and brown rudbeckia at the base, apricot and russety roses in the centre and apricot and cream freesia, including buds, at the top.

In the pink spray

A sheaf like the one opposite would make an unusual presentation on an informal occasion, or a suitable gift for a gardener to take a flat-dweller. It has the advantage of being all ready to stand in a deep container, a white jug or maybe decorative glass storage jar.

First of all, arrange the foliage flat on the table into an elongated fan-shape, tapering to a point at the top and with the greatest width two-thirds of the way down. Arrange the flowers on the leaves. Long-stemmed slender material comes first, to take the shape of the taper: we chose lavender here and in bunches at the sides. Then an arc of still smallish flowers that will neither look nor feel top-heavy, and have stems long enough to reach the water level. Ours are chive flowers. Next come bunches of scented old-fashioned pinks and sweet william. Pink alternates with white in the form of single cranesbill geranium and a scattering of small wild marguerites. Marjoram leaves flashed with gold are placed as side features and close to the grip.

Bind the posy with green twine and, if you like, with ribbon; but avoid flamboyant trailing bows, which would be out of keeping with a natural spray like this.

Stand the completed design in water until the last minute and wrap the stems in wet tissue and polythene in transit. Remember to dry the stems before the moment of presentation.

Presentation sprays need not be stiff and starchy. This one consists of lavender and chive flowers, pinks, sweet williams, cranesbill geranium and marguerites.

BOUQUET GARNI

Herbs are not only sweetly scented or pungently aromatic leaves, but the stuff of legends: history, folklore, old wives' tales, tradition, beliefs and disbeliefs – the essence of human life for centuries past.

In the Middle Ages herbs were used to strew floors and streets: an earth floor littered with dried stems of mint and thyme was considered preferable to the same surface neatly swept but malodorous. Probably the first 'arrangements' of herbs were the tussie-mussies first recorded by the seventeenth-century herbalist John Parkinson. These little scented nosegays, carefully chosen and decoratively arranged, often with a rose bud in the centre, were carried to mask unhygienic smells, and to be discreetly sniffed as an aid to warding off fevers and the plague. Such posies are still carried symbolically on ceremonial occasions, notably by judges.

In more recent times nosegays of herbs were composed to convey a special meaning, especially between lovers. Rosemary was for remembrance; angelica for inspiration; balm for sympathy; basil for courage; bay for constancy; chamomile for energy; coriander for hidden worth; fennel for strength; marjoram for blushes; mint for virtue; mugwort for happiness; parsley for merry-making; peppermint for warm feelings; rue for purification; sage for esteem and domestic virtue; and thyme for activity. Even today, little bunches of herbs can be assembled to convey a message.

Herbal rings and sheaves

You can make up evergreen herbs into charming circlets to hang in a kitchen. Practical yet too pretty to use, they make long-lasting gifts. Make a circle of wire – coat-hanger wire is ideal – and bind it with green tape; either bias binding or florist's tape will do. Using fuse wire, bind on small sprays of bay leaves, then partially cover them with clippings of rosemary and lavender. Small, short-stemmed bunches of lavender flowers and clusters of umbellifer seedheads picked at any stage of maturity are the finishing touches; choose from angelica, caraway, coriander, fennel, parsley, or what you will.

As an alternative, you can make a herb sheaf as a pretty wall decoration. Following the instructions on *page 34*, make a fan-shape of varying lengths of rosemary and cover them with stems of bay, lavender and illuminating bunches of purple sage. For the flowers, use lavender at the tip, then chives, clusters of dried chamomile and umbellifer seedheads to make the shape. To bind close to the grip you could make a little posy of single bay leaves surrounding ringlets of chamomile and chive flowers, with a raised dome of lavender in the centre. The instructions on *page 18* for making a spring-flower posy might be helpful.

A pot of herbs

A conventional arrangement of herbs makes a very welcome gift. The container can be part of it (the one opposite is a pottery half-pint tankard) or simply an unobtrusive holder such as a used mustard pot, a storage or preserve jar or similar.

It is possible to achieve this kind of arrangement without any stem-holding material, but if it is for a gift, and needs transporting, it is advisable to use something to keep it stable. If the journey is relatively short, fill the neck of the container with crumpled chicken wire (*see page 16*). Have water in the container until the last minute, tip it out for the trip, then remember to refill it on arrival. For a journey of, say, a couple of hours or more, it is best to fit the container with soaked foam, which will provide the stems with sustenance en route. Pack the container in a wide box and wedge it with rolls of newspaper.

The tallest stems, the angelica, are placed first, then the variegated lemon balm to the left, the sage to the right and the purple sage at the front. Long, full stems of dock seeds give visual weight back left, and buddleia, lavender and borage all lean into a right-hand bend.

The centre group is taken up with mint, golden marjoram and tarragon leaves and caraway, dill and angelica seedheads. White chamomile flowers provide the highlights and the golden yellow Jerusalem sage flower becomes the focal point. Fennel leaves throw a dark green spider's-web over the arrangement, linking the other materials.

Spot the herbs! The tankard is brim-full of angelica, lemon balm, sage, lavender, borage, mint, marjoram, tarragon, caraway, dill, chamomile and fennel.

WEDDING DISPLAY

Amid the flurry of preparations for a wedding, the person responsible for arranging the flowers in the church, reception hall and the bride's house has to tread the delicate path of an entrepreneur. The arrangements decorating each stage set for the bride must reflect the style of the occasion and the bride's own colour preference. Some weddings are unquestionably more formal than others, and certain flowers (lilies, alstroemeria, gladioli, irises, hot-house carnations, giant chrysanthemums and camellias, for example) are considered more appropriate for an elegant setting. Along with all the wild flowers, marguerites and other single, daisy-shaped types, pinks, love-in-a-mist, cornflowers, peonies and roses suit a country setting.

Pink flowers for the church and the reception hall win hands-down with today's brides – two to one over other colours, in my experience. But whilst the bride decides whether pink, yellow, blue, orange or cream flowers will best complement the colours being worn and carried by the bridal party, the flower-arranger must decide on the strength of those colours.

This means making a site visit. Take a notebook with you and note the colour and type of the background: whether the walls of the church are dark red brick or pale stone will determine whether pale or dark-coloured flowers will show up best. The strength and direction of the light will affect this decision too. For a pedestal in a corner that receives neither sunlight nor lamplight, play safe and go for the palest shades.

Take similar points into consideration in the reception room or hall. Plain curtains or plain-painted walls are the best possible backgrounds for flowers but can by no means be taken for granted. The more broken-up the background, with noticeboards, panels, strips of curtain, vertical timbers and so on, the more you will need to frame your arrangements with clean lines of foliage. See also the following pages.

Careful preparation

Preparation of the flowers is of prime importance. Frequently they need to be arranged on the day before the wedding; in summer the church, rooms or marquee might become hot and airless, and often the church flowers are to be left for Sunday's congregation to enjoy: a long stint.

Gather all the material the day before it is to be arranged, putting it immediately into buckets of water. Crush or split woody stems; singe sappy ones (*see page 26*); wrap tulips up to the neck in paper (*page 20*), cut all the stems under water (*page 16*), and leave all materials deep in water in a cool room overnight. *Never* rush out and gather more leaves or flowers to fill in gaps at the last minute. Those, without proper preparation, will be the ones that wilt.

Plan the flowers and foliage you need for all the arrangements as if they were ingredients for a wedding cake. You could even make a rough drawing of the containers, the proportion of each arrangement and a list of the components – three blue and five cream hyacinths, ten pale apricot tulips, two bunches of double narcissi, and so on.

Prepare the containers well in advance. Be sure they are secured even more carefully than usual with wire, florist's tape, string and so on, and keep the foam topped up with water.

The table pedestal

A triangular arrangement raised high on a tall vase is suitable for the centre of a buffet table or, standing on a side table, can take the place of a pedestal.

The container for the design opposite is a brass vase fitted with a 1-lb plastic margarine tub and half a block of soaked foam covered with chicken wire bound with florist's tape to the neck of the holder.

As with all triangular designs (*see page 42*), the top and two side points are placed first – sprays of viburnum and hawthorn respectively. Next come the tall pink spikes of *Orchis maderensis* and the pinks and pink alstroemeria outlining the sides. The centre is filled in with hawthorn, white lace-cap hydrangeas, pinks and a single pink rhododendron flower. This, the deepest pink of all the material, becomes the focal point and, with its ring of foliage, adequately covers the foam holder. For a romantic touch there are sprays of sheep's parsley, delicate as a wedding veil and prettily silhouetted against the lawn.

A pink and white colour scheme for a wedding is carried out in *Orchis maderensis*, pinks and alstroemeria with hawthorn, lace-cap hydrangeas and rhododendron.

GRACEFUL CURVES

Arranging flowers in church is a special privilege, giving us the opportunity to adorn a sacred and perhaps beautiful building. As a courtesy, before you make any plans, ask the clergyman's permission and at the same time ask whether there are any restrictions. For example, many priests do not allow flowers to be arranged on the high altar and some will not permit any arrangements beyond the communion rail. Also, check that the duty flower-arranger on the church rota if she is happy to have the job taken off her hands.

A low, curving display of flowers on a bench in the porch, or on a pedestal just inside the door, would be a welcoming sight for both bride and guests. A table or chest at the back of the church could take a flowing horizontal design. Niches or piscinas, and windowsills (as long as they are not too high and remote) are ideal locations. A pair of pedestals (page 42) on either side of the screen frames the proceedings beautifully.

Early on, plan how many arrangements to have and where they will be. Measure the height and width of any niches and windows, making sketches of the shapes. Measure the depth of the base or windowsill too: this will govern the size and type of container.

In niches and windows you could have a trailing triangular design in the centre or an L-shaped display to one side. Two niches or windows close together look well with back-to-back L-shaped arrangements; viewed together, they make an effective triangle. When decorating small windows, keep the designs reasonably low to avoid blocking out too much light.

If you are not an experienced flower-arranger, take a few boughs of foliage with you on your measuring-up session. Hold one upright and others along the base of a niche or window to trail over the edge and break up the horizontal line. Keep cutting them back until the proportions look just right.

Containers for church flowers are normally camouflaged and pass unnoticed. For the narrow base offered by niches and windowsills, old loaf-tins, rectangular foil baking dishes and plastic food-boxes are all suitable. You can spray-paint them with matt or emulsion paint to match the background colour. For downward-sloping stems, foam is likely to be the best stem-holder. Cut a large block, to extend about 5 cm (2 inches) above the container rim, soak it thoroughly and tape or tie it in place.

L-shaped designs

To make an L-shaped design, select some delicate foliage to form the upright and horizontal. Young oak leaves, lime, privet (golden privet if the background is dark), berberis, broom and rosemary are suitable.

Large, flat leaves are useful at the right angle and to give weight at the back of the design. Hostas (featured opposite), with their deep-ridged surface and intricate veining, are a perfect choice. Large ivy leaves or smaller ones used in groups, bergenia, geranium, arum, laurel or fig are other options. Hosta, bergenia and arum leaves must all be singed (*see page 26*) and should then be immersed rather than stood in water.

Possibilities for the flower points include stocks, as in our example, foxgloves, larkspur, clarkia, antirrhinums, astilbe, polygonum and freesias.

Full, round flowers give weight and balance through the centre. We chose three composite daisy shapes, with the constraint of only two colours: pink gerberas teamed with pink and white pyrethrums and white spray chrysanthemums. Roses teamed with day lily trumpets, carnations with alstroemeria, anemones with ranunculus, pom-pom dahlias with marigolds are all strong combinations, though your choice will be governed by the season and overall colour scheme.

In our design, the boughs of oak leaves were placed first: the upright, then the horizontal, then a short spray close to the right angle. Next came the stocks, following the same lines, then the foreground hosta leaf and three smaller ones, out of camera range, at the back. The five pink gerberas were placed, three in line and one to either side, then the pyrethrums between them, and lastly the white chrysanthemums were tucked into the natural curve of the hosta leaf.

As you build up a design, keep backing away from it so that you can assess it from a distance and adjust accordingly. Before you leave, top up the water in the container to keep the foam moist, and spray the flowers with a fine shower of water from an atomizer.

To outline a stone niche in a church,
the L-shaped design is framed by young
pale green oak and hosta leaves and filled in
with pink pyrethrums, gerberas
and spray chrysanthemums.

HIGH ON A PEDESTAL

Glorious displays of flowers lifted high on wooden, iron or marble stands, 'pedestals' typify traditional English flower design and are seen to greatest effect in church, large reception rooms or other public places where they can be viewed at a distance.

Usually the regular, flowing lines of a triangular shape are best for a single pedestal, tall in the centre of the design and curving gracefully well below the level of the actual container. When a pair of pedestals is placed, for instance, on each side of the chancel steps or framing a fireplace, an asymmetrical or irregular triangle can be more interesting, with the steep, more upright angle on the inside and freer, more flowing lines at the outer edges.

Before deciding on the shape and proportion of a pedestal design, view the location, take or seek out the pedestal you will be using, and decide there and then, with the aid of some long branches of leaves, on the most effective height and width for your design. Assess the proportion from a distance, too, and check the lighting and background.

Stand-fitting

For the container, use something like a large, flat bowl or baking dish about 25 cm (10 inches) in diameter; the condition is not important, as it will not show. It is worth buying pinholders with widely spaced spikes, specially made to hold foam firmly in place: there will be quite a weight of stems and flowers at the end.

Press a small blob of OasisFix, water-resistant clay, on to the base of each pinholder and press them into the container. For large arrangements, stand a whole block of soaked foam on end at the back of the container with another one cut into two in front. Press the foam into the spikes, then cover it with a piece of crumpled chicken wire pulled up to form a dome. Tuck the ends of the wire inside the container rim, then tie it in place parcel-fashion. Tie or tape the whole container to the top of the pedestal so that it is absolutely rigid. Keep the foam wet.

Possible 'fillers' include pale green and fluffy alchemilla mollis or, in winter, hellebores, otherwise bridal white pyrethrum parthenium, cow parsley, sheep's parsley or gypsophila, clusters of old-fashioned pinks, sprays of deutzia or choisya, elderflower, what you will.

Creating the pedestal design

Allow seven pieces of the main, longer-stemmed foliage: one for the main central feature and one slightly shorter, just in front of it; two pieces curving down low, one to the right and one to the left of the design; two of middle height to stand upright, one on each side within the confines of the triangular shape; and one, cut shorter, to trail low over the front of the container. To conceal the container, and to tuck in among the low-level flowers, you will probably need eight to ten of the flat leaves – perhaps more in winter to eke out expensive blooms.

Flowers are usually calculated in uneven numbers, generally assuming one in the centre with the others divided equally on each side. Five or seven stems of the main pointed material with three or five stems of secondary points (gladioli and stocks in our church pedestal), three or five large round flowers for the main feature, 15 to 17 smaller round flowers in varying colours, and a collection of filling-in material would do for an arrangement like the one opposite.

Strip off unwanted leaves from flower stems and all the lower leaves from stems of foliage. Play safe by flame-singeing *all* flower and foliage stems. Scrape off 5 cm (2 inches) of the bark from woody stems, gently crush them or split the ends. Store the material in buckets of water; for travelling, pack them in boxes lined with damp newspaper.

You will need a large sheet of polythene to protect the floor, secateurs, scissors, a watering-can with a long spout and a fine-mist atomizer to spray the finished arrangement (a laundry spray is ideal).

Place the long-stemmed foliage first, then the flower 'points' that follow the same lines. Place the upright stems at the side, then position the central flowers, some recessed into the design and others projecting well forward: at all costs avoid a flat look. Fill in with smaller flowers and delicate 'filler' material such as sheep's parsley, but do not overcrowd the design. Neaten the sides and back.

The pinnacle of floral art, and very typically English, a pedestal design sets the scene in church. A triangular shape is easier than a random one to achieve.

LUCKY WHITE HEATHER

Not all pedestal arrangements require masterly organiz-ation and *carte blanche* in a well-stocked garden. For a homely wedding party you can create a beautiful table centrepiece on a pretend pedestal, using the minimum of flowers to delightful effect.

Create your own mini pedestal from a glass, china or pottery cake stand – still one of the cheap and cheerful treasures worth looking out for in junk shops. Cake stands have flat tops, usually with a raised lip all round, whilst their close cousins, ham or bacon stands, are slightly dish-shaped.

Soaked foam is the best form of stem holder for this design, as you will want many of the stems to slant sharply downwards. At this angle they could never reach the water in a container. Secure either a plastic foam-holding saucer or a special pinholder to the stand with blobs of water-resistant florist's clay, and then position the foam. A small cylinder or one-third of a rectangular block will be enough.

Our arrangement for a spring wedding (opposite) uses a single bunch of mixed narcissi in yellow and cream and three stems of yellow spray chrysanthemums. The extras are spotted laurel leaves, lime-green cupressus, variegated periwinkle foliage, long sprays of pale yellow mahonia, japonica just bursting into flower, and lucky white heather.

Circular designs

This arrangement was designed for the centre of a round buffet-table. For this purpose, walk slowly round your finished display checking that it does not show a 'wrong' side.

The periwinkle leaves – each stem singed the day before – are placed first, three upright in the centre and seven trailing over the rim all around. Other stems are cut short so that the cream and green variegated leaves are pressed close against the foam. The spotted laurel leaves and sprays of cupressus are inserted at different heights and three-quarters or side face, where they will separate and project the flowers.

Fully-open narcissi are used for 'weight' around the rim with the buds tapering off towards the top. The largest chrysanthemums are cut off on their short stems and placed low down. The buds stay on the long stems for height. Spikes of mahonia pierce the groups of flowers and heather is used as a filler.

Material for a large pedestal

When you are designing a large pedestal (such as the one on *page 43*) a rough sketch (*see page 38*) will help you select the flowers and cut branches to outline the shape. A very slight curve is acceptable in the tallest central stem; those outlining the angles to left and right need to have clearly defined natural curves in each direction. Sprays of young, pale, bright green oak or beech leaves are effective: in winter you can use chestnut brown branches of the same materials preserved in glycerine. Long, curved brown stems of stephandra tanakae are effective with cream, apricot or bronze schemes; for a green, yellow and white theme the variegated leaves of eleagnus pungens or aralia elata would be suitable. For a spring wedding consider branches of apple, pear or cherry blossom, or long, dainty stems of broom.

Use some large, flat leaves to conceal the container, give balance at the sides and counter-balance at the back of the design. Hosta, bergenia, arum and large ivy leaves are all suitable. Rhododendron, azalea or hydrangea flowers cut with an encircling cluster of leaves are attractive low-level features.

For the flowers, choose first 'points', long-stemmed and sharply pointed material that follows the line of the tall foliage in creating the top and side angles. Among the possibilities are gladioli, foxgloves, del-phinium, Canterbury bells, larkspur, verbascum, antir-rhinum, lilies, lilac and stocks.

For the central features you need round flowers such as roses, carnations, dahlias, chrysanthemum, camellias and so on. Tulips are useful, as they can be placed at the sides, to be seen in silhouette, and in the centre to be viewed full-face and 'round'.

A cake-stand-cum-pedestal makes a splash with the minimum of flowers, a bunch of yellow and cream narcissi and three stems of spray chrysanthemums.

EATING AL FRESCO

Arranging flowers for the garden might seem like taking coals to Newcastle. But think of barbecue parties on the patio, a picnic on the lawn, a summer wedding or christening reception in a marquee, or just having a few friends in for a drink under the sun or stars. And then look at the garden critically, as you would at a room where you were going to hold a party.

The chances are that there will be an area of the garden that could do with a bit of a lift. Perhaps you need a focal point on the terrace or in the porch, or maybe a long fence could do with an island of colour.

That is where portable flower arrangements come in: anywhere the garden needs them. For outdoor entertaining, it really pays to be pessimistic. It is no use gazing up at the benign sky and opting for a fragile, tottery container that will falter at the slightest puff of wind. Instead, be prepared for a good, stiff breeze and choose a container with a firm, wide base. Garden trugs are ideal: our choice was a practical souvenir of a holiday in the Dordogne. Traditional Sussex trugs and willow baskets are other natural choices. Galvanized buckets can be surprisingly fetching once there are a few leaves trailing over the rim. Old saucepans and cooking pots, large casseroles and bread crocks also serve the purpose well. Plastic containers are never so 'sympathetic' outdoors.

If the container is on the tall side, weight it by half-filling it with sand or stones before topping up with water or inserting foam. That way it will stay firm no matter what the vagaries of the weather, or how excited children or animals become.

Ensure that any holding materials you use are firmly secured to the container: wire netting wired or tied round the rim or to a handle, foam wedged into the aperture and taped or tied to the pot. Make these precautions part of your routine; do a double check for flowers in public places or outdoors.

Choice of flowers
Choose flowers that are in keeping with the mood or style of the occasion. For a barbecue party you could echo the colours of the burning embers in the flowers, using seasonal flowers in flame, coral and brilliant reds. Zinnias, dahlias and chrysanthemums all glow with vibrant colour.

For a wedding or christening party, the flowers should follow the colour theme of the day. If the bridesmaids are wearing pink, go for deep cyclamen shades and sugar-almond tones blended with white or cream, which will look both romantic and pretty. If it is a case of blue for a boy you might have to cheat and blend some mauve asters, dahlias or michaelmas daisies with the blues of borage, alkanet, larkspur, according to the season. Spike the blues and mauves with cream and white and touches of gold for maximum impact.

Never fall into the trap of choosing flowers that are too small to be seen at a distance or too pale and insignificant to hold their own in a crowd. And if the party is to linger on into twilight, be sure to include more than a smattering of light-coloured blooms. Dark flowers blend all too soon into the gathering dusk and a stunning display of velvety reds, blues and purples will have disappeared completely long after paler shades are still shining like beacons.

The garden trug
The flower arrangement shown opposite was designed not to look like an arrangement at all, but as if the collection of spray chrysanthemums had just been cut from the border and placed there.

This particular trug was heavy and needed no weighting, but a light garden basket would need one or two heavy stones. The base of the trug was lined with plastic sheeting to stop the moisture seeping into the wood – a not altogether necessary precaution for a garden accessory. About two-thirds of a block of soaked green Oasis foam was stood on end on the left-hand side and firmly taped in position, from back to front and side to side.

The arrangement is simple. Place the longest stems first, to determine the length of the design, then cut short those that are to outline the shape – vaguely, that of a fan. Cut some of the shortest side stems and press the flowers close to the foam to conceal it. Then fill in the design, alternating dark and light colours and aiming to keep it casual.

A sturdy wooden trug filled with a bunch of spray chrysanthemums, just as they were cut.

COLOUR PORTABLE

Fashions change in floral art as in clothes and furnishings – and indeed these are all closely linked. Today, preferences tend to be for flower arrangements using only two or three adjacent or complementary colours, but this is a matter of choice. There are no hard and fast rules. How can there be, when a herbaceous border or a bed of annuals in every imaginable colour looks so naturally right?

The terms 'adjacent' and 'complementary', when used in relation to colour, have specific meanings. As a simple guide, the colours may be divided into six groups or families and arranged in a circle in precisely the same order as they appear in the rainbow – a natural colour guide. Red is at the top, as in the rainbow. Miss one section and you come to blue; after the next comes yellow. These three primary colours alternate with (1) violet (a mixture of red and blue, therefore placed between them; (2) green, between blue and yellow; and (3) orange, between yellow and red.

When white is mixed with any colour, this is called a tint of the pure colour; when grey is mixed with a colour it becomes a tone, and with the addition of black it is called a shade. White, grey and black are referred to as neutrals.

When colours – or tints, tones or shades of those colours – that are next to each other on the colour wheel are used together, the design is called adjacent. One example is the blend of yellow buttercups and green spurge in the 'meadow-sweet' design on *page 29*; another is the bowl of red and orange autumn blooms on *page 61*. In both, the colours featured are close together on the wheel.

Colours are termed complementary when they are opposite each other on the wheel. The primroses and violets in the spring nosegay on *page 19* show how attractive these opposites can be. Blue and orange or red and green are other complementary pairings.

When alternating colours are grouped together they are termed triadic. Red and blue anemones, blue and yellow hyacinths, or yellow and red dahlias all illustrate this point.

Whilst there is no need to restrict your designs to adjacent, complementary or triadic colour groupings,

it can sometimes be useful to bear them in mind when building up your arrangements. For instance, if you have one beautiful red peony or a cluster of three red rhododendron flowers that you want to show to full advantage, place them next to material in their complementary colour on the wheel – green. A ring of foliage, a cluster of green hellebore flowers or stems of lime green tobacco plants will all throw the spotlight on to the red focal-point flowers. Violet or orange flowers, on the other hand, the adjacent colours to red on the wheel, would detract from their glory.

The multi-coloured group

A hand-thrown pottery urn in natural earthy brown holds the gamut of high-summer flower hues. The neck of the container is filled with crumpled chicken wire to hold the stems. The only ones that droop low over the rim are those with a built-in natural curve: some of the sweet peas, for example, are almost U-shaped and easily reach into the water.

Starting at the top of the colour wheel, if not quite at the tip of the design, there are red pyrethrums, single daisy-shaped composite flowers and sweet peas in tints of red mixed with varying amounts of white. Representing violet on the wheel are the full, voluptuous heads of night-scented stock, in a pale tint of mauve. Move one section further round on the wheel, to blue, and you come to the wild alkanet, clusters of richly-coloured flowers on decidedly wayward stems (another candidate for singeing, but despite such pre-conditioning the stems often wilt).

Green, next in order, is confined to a few leaves and the pale ice-green of some unopened elderflowers. However, green is represented by the background of the leafy glade.

Yellow features in the pyrethrum and marguerite centres and, in its palest form, in the cream of the tree lupins and elderflowers. Tints of orange, coming full circle, are evident in the coral sweet peas.

The woody stems of elderflowers should be scraped and crushed or split at the ends and then singed or dipped in boiling water. The pale green, under-developed stems should be singed.

A design for an outdoor party, featuring in turn every beautiful colour of the rainbow, proves that where flowers and colour are concerned, anything goes.

ROSE GARDEN

For Sunday lunch or late, late supper in the garden, a flowing bowl or casual cluster of blowsy roses is just right. Now is the time to wander through the rose garden or border cutting a selection of exuberant, fully-opened flowers. Apricot and coral, cyclamen and pink, cream and white, together they look marvellous.

As for the container, if it is a smart party, bring on the crystal rose-bowl, polish up the family silver, or take the wraps off a stored-away wedding present. But if the mood is informal and carefree, go for something with an outdoor feel.

The 'container' does not actually have to contain anything at all: witness the piece of blue coral in the photograph opposite, rippled like fossilized sand and sparkling like frost on a hedgerow. Less of a container, more an accessory, the coral is fitted with a piece of soaked holding foam firmly strapped to one end with water-resistant tape. The stems are pushed in as if they are growing straight out of this great barrier reef, and the trickery is concealed by judiciously placed shiny rose leaves and a low cluster of white floribunda roses.

Another way to create such an effect is to place a small jar or pot in a curve of the coral (this piece has several), fit it with foam if the design needs it, and hide the container behind trailing flowers and leaves.

Shell-holders

Continuing the seashore theme, shells of all kinds make wonderful flower-holders. Large, cone-shaped triton shells, spiralled like a cream horn, can become natural cornucopias spilling over with pink and white wild roses, garden pinks and sea holly or the silvery leaves of santolina or *Cineraria maritima*.

For a long-lasting arrangement, wedge the neck of the shell with dry foam and arrange the pretty immortelles – pink and white *Helipterum manglesii*, white and yellow-domed winged everlasting, long stems of golden *Helichrysum angustifolium*, with the purple-striped seed-heads of love-in-a-mist, bluish urns of poppy heads, and that fluffiest of grasses, *Lagurus ovatus*, or hare's-tail.

Scallop, oyster, and large mussel shells make surprisingly pretty containers for small arrangements of both fresh and dried flowers. Just tape a scrap of foam into the centre, then turn a few flower and foliage snippings into individual designs to put on display, maybe one at each place round the dinner-table, or give as pretty gifts.

Handfuls of pebbles can be used, like marbles, as stem-holders: they are especially suitable in a glass bowl or jug, where the mechanics show. Lower the stones in gently to avoid cracking the glass, fill the container with water and push the stems down between them. They will be held securely and decoratively in a vice-like grip.

A spot of beachcombing could provide you with an interestingly gnarled and knobbly piece of driftwood. Failing that, florists sell these fantastically-shaped pieces of natural sculpture quite cheaply.

The size and shape of the wood will suggest the design. Conceal the container behind the wood and arrange the flowers so that they look as if they are growing over and around it – in other words, make sure the wood is an integral part of the scheme, not just a bystander. Brilliant yellow daffodils and deep ocean-blue hyacinths; sky-blue and sun-gold meconopsis with trails of ivy; blue, mauve, yellow and white irises, fiercely mauve-pink semi-double Regensberg floribundas with entwining trails of mixed *Rosa rugosa* – these are the striking colour blends I like to see against the neutral dappled grey of the wood.

Large, flattish pieces of weather-bleached wood, slabs of granite and pieces of slate all come in to play as natural 'plate' containers. The easiest way to fit them is to have a plastic 'saucer' of foam at one end and make a flowing arc or L-shaped arrangement of twigs, branches and flowers. Pussy willow twigs and yellow spring bulbs; apple blossom and deep pink pyrethrums; or in winter bronze berberis, green stinking hellebores and waxy Christmas roses, they make the most of *objets trouvés*. To cover the mechanics, a handful of sphagnum moss, pebbles, gravel or tiny shells would all be appropriate.

An intricate piece of blue coral is a lovely foil for a cluster of summer roses in warm tones of pink and apricot. The stems are held in foam.

ROMANTIC AIR

When a party in the garden has romantic overtones – the celebration of an engagement, a young girl's coming of age, a wedding or a christening – the occasion calls not for a weighty wooden trug of worthy blooms or a camouflaged bucket of bulbs, but for designs that are delicate and pretty. Yet they should be eye-catching in a crowd: almost a paradox.

You may want to brighten up a corner of the terrace, place something worth looking at towards the end of a garden path or draw attention away from the less-than-lovely features all gardens have. Before deciding what type of displays will look best, consider the colour of the backgrounds: arrangements bulked out with a flurry of foliage will make little impact against the green of the grass or the brown of the toolshed.

White is a good choice for containers, showing up well against grass, earth and paving and still glowing like a beacon as darkness falls.

A few large designs will make far more impact, and be less work, than several small ones, so it is worth borrowing a selection of huge white wash-stand jugs and bowls. With their clean, uncluttered lines and enormous capacity, they are guaranteed to stand out in a crowd. Alternatively, use large flower-pots sprayed with white emulsion paint (preferably two coats) and fitted with foam or given inner water-holding liners.

From hothouse and hedgerow

White is also a good choice for the majority of the flowers, blended with just one or two strong colours. For a coming-of-age celebration in a country garden, an almost entirely green background of grass and shrubs, our idea was to import sheep's parsley, or Queen Anne's lace, from the hedgerow and fill the jugs to overflowing. Sugar-icing-pink campion growing alongside was, as it happened, a perfect match for the glorious gerberas in the greenhouse. Pink pyrethrums, single spray chrysanthemums, roses, carnations and sweet williams would be less exotic alternatives.

If a wayside walk is not practical, you could achieve this froth-of-white effect with clouds of sea lavender and gypsophila, from florists or flower barrows, or emulate it with Russian vine or creamy-white astilbe.

Pretty as it is for free-standing arrangements in the garden, this mophead effect looks somewhat untidy for a table centrepiece. Make the designs mix and match by reversing the colour balance, and arranging a more conventional grouping of the pink flowers spattered with mere wisps of the sheep's parsley. A simpler version of the design on *page 39* would be lovely.

Hanging baskets

If yours is a patio or balcony party and space is at a premium, you can hang the flower decorations attractively and conveniently out of the way. A tree trunk, corner post or even a clothes-line post can support a hanging basket overflowing with cut flowers.

Use shallow woven baskets, large plastic food tubs (spray-painted) or, if you have them, ordinary hanging baskets. Line them with damp sphagnum moss and push in blocks of soaked holding foam – a more efficient medium. Beg, borrow or buy the prettiest selection of trailers you can find – miniature variegated ivy leaves, clematis foliage and flowers or, better still, the wild and woolly seedheads of the old man's beard, fragrant spikes of buddleia, honeysuckle, wisteria, what you will.

Arrange the trailing foliage and flowers all around so that they virtually cover the container, then make a cushion of flowers, bringing the design into the gentle curves of a dome in the centre.

The flower jug

The wash-stand jug opposite is fitted at the top with a ball of crumpled mesh chicken wire, tucked neatly inside the rim and, to stop it wobbling, taped criss-cross over the top with water-resistant tape. Ten pink gerberas facing in all directions begin the design, their stems of varying heights. It is important to arrange one short-stemmed flower on each side to break the line of the rim and link the container with the plant materials. A profusion of sheep's parsley is arranged next and, as it is a wild flower, allowed to display a certain waywardness. The pink campion tucked among the white flowers forms a perfect link between the showy greenhouse blooms and the dainty wildings.

With a mass of sheep's parsley or cow parsley from the wayside, or minute-flowered gypsophila, you can make a lovely impact with a few special blooms.

WEDDING ANNIVERSARIES

Choosing and arranging flowers as a wedding-anniversary gift or to decorate the party room is an immensely satisfying task. By the time you have taken account of the couple's favourite flowers, perhaps a sentimental attachment to the ones the bride carried in her bouquet, and the designation of the year in question (crystal for 15 years of wedded bliss and coral after 35, for example), you are left with the thrill of a fascinating puzzle. With luck, you may be able to combine the happy couple's chosen flowers in the appropriate colour for the occasion, or arrange them in a container made of the appropriate material.

For just as there is a traditional and sentimental language of flowers handed down and undoubtedly added to over the generations, so there is a special designation for each wedding anniversary: at least, for each one up to the first fifteen years. After that the list goes up in five-year leaps and bounds.

Sometimes the designation suggests a colour theme for the flowers: coral at 35; ruby after 40 years; sapphire (other than blue) for 45; gold for 50 years; emerald at 55; diamond (white) at 60, and blue sapphire after 65 years.

More often the occasion is marked by a material, which could be represented by the container or even the background on which the flowers are placed. After the first year of marriage a bowl of red roses, signifying undying love, could be sct to good effect on a dainty broderie anglaise tablecloth to represent the cotton called for by the occasion.

In year seven it is wool: perhaps one of granny's old crochet shawls could be pressed into service to cover the table. By year 12 the theme is silk and fine linen, and in year 13 it is lace. It would be a charming idea to pin a few lace flowers among fresh blooms in an arrangement or to tie a presentation sheaf with a lace ribbon bow.

The second year of marriage is marked by paper, which presents many possibilities. You could form a Victorian circlet posy inside a scalloped paper doily, in just the way they did at the turn of the century; make a breath-taking display of bold and beautiful red, orange and yellow Mexican paper poppies (which have the added advantage of immortality); or turn the problem on its head and use a papier mâché container. A brightly coloured jar, bowl or lidded box would look lovely with a clutch of white wild or garden flowers. (Protect the container by using an inner liner, or wrap soaked foam in foil or polythene.)

Year three calls for leather – perhaps a gift of a leather jug or tankard adorned with flowers or, for a bride of three years, a surprise gift of a soft leather belt colour-keyed to the flowers and tied in a bow around a low-key container.

Wood, copper, bronze, pottery, tin, steel, ivory; as you go through the list on *page 58* you will find more clues to help you choose containers and accessories and make wedding-anniversary flower arrangements through the years delightfully specific to each occasion.

Pot of roses

Whether the married couple's favourite flowers are roses, or they are celebrating their silver or ruby wedding, the arrangement on the *facing page* wins hands down. It is the sort of informal happy-family design that would look at home in the centre of a tea or supper table – and smell divine.

It is advisable not to use crumpled wire as the stem-holder in containers of precious metal, in case of scratching. Either fill the neck with soaked foam or – as we did here, since roses seem to prefer it – place the stems directly in the water. In this case, tape around the inside of the neck with water-resisting tape to protect it from any rose thorns.

Then arrange the tallest stems first, criss-crossing them as much as the limited space allows, so that they make a mesh to hold firm the ones that follow.

Single dog roses, clusters of floribundas, rich double musk roses and old-fashioned climbers – here is a display to gladden the hearts of any couple with something to celebrate.

A silver container flatters any group of flowers and many occasions besides silver wedding anniversaries, and red roses, signifying love, always have romantic connotations.

REFLECTED GLORY

Stand a display of flowers on a polished metal tray and suddenly the whole group comes to life, as the shapes and colours are reflected like lilies in a pool. This is a winning way to make the most of a limited selection of blooms, as the tray becomes part of the design and visually enlarges the whole group.

Specially appropriate of course for a silver wedding, a tray in silver plate rises to any occasion. Whether it carries a sunburst of early spring flowers, as in the design *opposite*, or a child's collection of miniature wild flowers, it makes a positive statement of celebration.

Wedding anniversary designations offer other opportunities for gleaming trays of flowers. After seven years it is copper. Rarely appreciated as beautiful accessories, copper trays turn up at very low prices in junk- and second-hand shops. Imagine a display with coral-and-cream-speckled alstroemeria, palest pink carnations, blackberry leaves and sprays of preserved foliage; or a group of fruit and flowers in pale green and apricot with a pineapple, stinking hellebores, 'white' grapes and coral rosebuds. So tempting, it would be hard to part with the tray as part of the gift! Incidentally, fruit and flowers together are the theme for wedding anniversary number four.

Eighth wedding anniversaries are celebrated with the help of bronze. Again, you could base the design on a tray, or use a bronze figurine as an accessory beside an arrangement. Clear lemon yellow, cream and green schemes have an affinity with this metal, carried out with, say, yellow gladioli spikes, molucella, or bells of Ireland, narcissi and tulips and the linking colours of variegated eleagnus foliage.

Tin and steel, for years ten and eleven, seem less sympathetic metals to grace such important occasions. But a painted tin tray or a stainless steel dish can be a good foil for an arrangement. For the tray, choose a plain colour or one with the simplest of designs – perhaps just a decorative edging – to avoid detracting from the flowers. Red, blue, yellow or any of the colours in between give great scope for designs in adjacent, complementary or triadic colours (*see page 48*).

You have to work harder with the polishing cloth to see your flowers in a tray made of wood (year five), but both old and new ones can make most effective backgrounds, especially for an arrangement of dried flowers: an everlasting memento of a happy occasion.

Loading the tray

Using the tray as a base, you need a suitable container for the holding foam. A plastic saucer made for the purpose is ideal on a wooden or painted tin tray, but does not look too impressive reflected in metal. A small china or pottery bowl in an insignificant colour is preferable.

In this kind of container, fix a special pinholder inside the bowl with a dab or two of florist's clay, OasisFix, then push the soaked foam on to the widely-spaced spikes. The foam-holding saucer, of course, needs no such extra security.

Place the container well to one side of the tray and secure it with a dab or two of Plasticine. Do not use OasisFix here. It can be messy to remove and may leave a smear on the surface.

To achieve a pleasing proportion in either a symmetrical or an asymmetrical flower design in relation to its tray or base, the longest stem should be at least one-and-a-half times the measurement of the widest part of the tray. In the design opposite, that relates to the tallest spikes of gladioli buds.

The fan-shape of gladioli and freesias is positioned first, then the backing cupressus foliage and the sprays covering the container. With the largest bloom used as a central and focal point, the carnations are placed next, with the mimosa placed last of all as a deliciously scented filler.

An elegant choice for a golden or silver wedding anniversary, a fan-burst of gladioli buds, freesias, scented carnations and mimosa, arranged on a silver tray.

RED ROSES

With all their romantic connotations, red roses are especially appropriate for wedding anniversary gifts and arrangements – but particularly so, of course, to celebrate a ruby wedding: 40 years of marriage. No one knows who first decided, or when, that deep red roses signify true love, or that red rose buds are the prerogative of a young girl as a token from her lover. But old habits die hard, and more roses are given as sentimental tokens than any other flower.

Treated with the loving care they deserve, these flowers should remain in good condition for a reasonable length of time. Many roses bought from florists will have been grown in hothouses and have experienced quite a temperature shock on emerging; others are imported, and reach the shops and markets only after a long journey. Whatever the circumstances, they will need a long reviving drink, deep in tepid water, before they are put on show.

Treatment of roses

As with all other flowers, strip off all the foliage, or at least those leaves that will come below the water line. There may be some you want to leave on for effect, but as a general rule it is best to use stems of foliage which have been treated separately.

Re-cut the stems under water, making a steeply diagonal cut with a pair of sharp secateurs to expose the maximum area for taking up water. Strip off the thorns, not only for safety's sake. They can cause a tangle as you arrange the stems with other materials.

Roses come into the category of woody-stemmed plant materials and as such need a helping hand to facilitate the water take-up, which is what keeping flowers fresh is all about. Scrape off the bark from the last 5 cm (2 inches) at the base of the stem. Then lightly crush each stem end with a hammer (and it must be lightly) or split it with secateurs or a sharp knife.

Gather the roses into a bunch, wrap paper round the heads to protect them and dip the stems in shallow boiling water for a few seconds. Then leave them in a bucket of water in a cool room – overnight, if time permits.

Before arranging the flowers, dip the heads in cool (not icy cold) water for a minute or so. And as you cut the stems to position them, do this in the usual (professional) way – under water. Spray the flowers with water after arranging and at daily intervals.

The table centre

The design photographed opposite is built up on a glass candlestick. As crystal signifies fifteen years of marriage, it would be particularly appropriate for that anniversary. Tall and elegant though the design is, it uses only half-a-dozen red roses, a bunch of mixed-colour freesias, stems of winter jasmine and garden foliage.

Treat the woody-stemmed foliage – the rhododendron, eleagnus, mahonia and sage – as you do the roses. Ivy is too good-tempered to need it. Singe the stem ends of periwinkle.

Fit the candlestick with a candle-cup holder, or its equivalent, and a cylinder of wet foam (*see page 12*).

Arrange the tallest stems, of jasmine, roses and freesias, first. Then position the central foliage, roses and freesias. Position the low-slanting side materials, then fill in with generous sprays of foliage – alternating matt and shiny, grey and yellowy – at the sides, and the back.

Wedding anniversary checklist

As the years go by, you can check off the list and choose flowers or containers appropriate to the occasion.

Year	Designated by	Year	Designated by
1	Cotton	14	Ivory
2	Paper	15	Crystal
3	Leather	20	China
4	Fruit and flowers	25	Silver
5	Wood	30	Pearl
6	Candy or sweets	35	Coral
7	Wool or copper	40	Ruby
8	Bronze or pottery	45	Sapphire (other than blue)
9	Pottery or willow	50	Gold
10	Tin	55	Emerald
11	Steel	60	Diamond
12	Silk and fine linen	65	Blue sapphire
13	Lace		

Arranging flowers high up on a tall container, such as a glass candlestick, gives them extra impact. Half-a-dozen red rosebuds are here blended with freesias and winter jasmine.

HARVEST HOME

When the harvest is safely gathered in and the gulls are swooping noisily among the furrows in the wake of the plough, the hedgerows and gardens are full of sun-bronzed flowers, ripening berries and reddening leaves.

With all this autumn bounty, it is a joy to arrange flowers for the traditional harvest festival services in church, polish up fruit and vegetables to take as a harvest offering and look out a few pots of mellow preserves to add to the array. Surely the churches never look lovelier than in these golden days.

It is a marvellous season, too, for flower arrangements in the home. There is an extra-precious quality about the last lingering, hardy blooms of autumn. Gather them before they are touched by the icy chill of winter, and place them in a window, where they can bask in the low, slanting rays of the sun.

Autumn leaves

Cutting branches of golden autumn leaves to arrange can bring disappointments as well as joy. If the leaves are at an advanced stage, and just about to fall off the trees, they will soon shed their foliage once they are cut – and leave gaping voids in your arrangements.

To have a good selection of russety leaves that will see you through many an autumn, plan ahead. Cut leaves in the early summer, while the sap is still rising in the trees and shrubs, and preserve the branches in a solution of glycerine. That way they will take on something akin to their autumn cloaks of many colours, and remain supple and pliable into the bargain. For instructions, *see page 86.*

For a shorter-term expedient, press fallen autumn leaves between the pages of old telephone directories or between newspapers under the carpet.

Look to the deeply cut and richly coloured scarlet oak and the chestnut tones of shumard oak; the bright yellow, tulip-shaped whitewood and the irresistibly golden Norway maple; the burning-bright American smoketree and the green-cum-scarlet multi leaves of the rowan; the purplish shades of common mulberry or the long, slender cream fingers of willow to add shape and invigorating colour to your designs.

Once the leaves are pressed it is a very simple

matter, using twists of fuse wire, to wire them to dried stems to mix and mingle with fresh or dried flowers. Larger pressed leaves, like London plane, maple and horse chestnut, can be fixed to thick-gauge florist's stub wires, which then act as false stems. (Buy the wires in bundles from florists or floral art clubs.) These leaves make attractive cover-ups, strategically placed over foam, saucers, wire and other paraphernalia.

November glory

All the materials in the autumn arrangement opposite were gathered on one glorious November day, except for some sprays of pre-pressed rowan leaves.

The group brings together all that is loveliest about the season, the brilliant colours of show chrysanthemums, generous sprays of single chrysanthemums perfectly toning with Enchantment lilies from the greenhouse and intermingled with rose hips, cotoneaster, hawthorn, rowan and black privet fruits. A few summer flowers have brazened their way into autumn: coral, pink and white antirrhinums and pert little marigolds, more appreciated now than ever. To contrast with all this brilliance, there are dried hops, pale, earthy brown and useful as fillers.

Working the design

The container is a straight-sided pottery jug and, as such, asymmetrical. This suggests an irregular (some say lopsided) triangular design for the arrangement. The jug is fitted with a shallow plate, slightly larger than the aperture, holding half a rectangular block of soaked foam. Because of the length of stems and weight of the flowers, a piece of wire mesh netting is wrapped over the foam for safety and the whole criss-cross taped to the container.

The tallest stems, of spray chrysanthemums, are placed first, then the lowest ones, the antirrhinum and the pyracanthus berries, on each side. Each side is outlined from the centre top downwards, with berries, chrysanthemums and lilies marking the shape. Then the centre line is filled in with lilies, foliage and the scarlet flowers that form the focal point. Marigolds and hops are used as fillers.

Accessories can add a great deal of visual 'weight' to flower designs. The jars of preserves emphasize the harvest theme of this late-summer group.

VEGETABLE BASKET

Zingy red peppers and tomatoes, cool green marrows and calabrese, mysterious purple aubergines and red cabbage, parchment-cream parsnips and mushrooms, warm orange pumpkin and carrots – a heaven-sent collection of materials for harvest thanksgiving.

If you are involved in decorating the church for the festival, who arranges what and where will probably be a committee decision. Perhaps you will be asked to design a display for one or two windowsills, fill a niche, decorate the top of an oak linen chest or make a flight of steps the focus of attention. Other people will bring individual offerings, perhaps a prize marrow, a plate of eggs, a posy of marigolds, a pot or two of jam, and add them to the display: a heartening example of community spirit.

For this reason, because a medley of other produce is likely to be placed alongside the planned arrangements, it is advisable to make your designs flexible. Ones with a gentle curve, an irregular shape and flowing lines rather than geometric precision are preferable. The jug of autumn flowers and bright berry fruits on *page 61* looks well with the addition of the preserve jars in their bright little gingham mob caps. Small pots of marigold posies, a pat of farm butter or a freshly baked loaf would only strengthen the effect.

If you have a productive vegetable garden or are likely to be tempted by the autumn plenty of a street market, a basket of vegetables makes a decorative and useful gift. You will find preparing this display just as fulfilling and rewarding as arranging flowers, the only danger being that the result may look too good to eat.

A matter of contrasts

Follow some of the same guidelines you take into account when selecting plant materials and try to achieve a balance of shiny and matt surfaces, rich, deep colours and less emphatic ones, large round shapes and tiny fillers: a handful of brussels sprouts or button mushrooms, for example, can be tucked in anywhere.

Wash and polish all the smooth-skinned vegetables until they shine – red, green and yellow peppers, marrows, courgettes, aubergines and tomatoes. If you include fruit as well, spruce up apples and pears but wash and dry plums and gages carefully so that they keep their bloom – it is part of their natural charm.

Strip any damaged and discoloured outer leaves from cabbages and sprouts and strip off the enveloping leaves of cauliflowers to expose the heart. Strip off some but not all of the covering leaves from heads of sweetcorn to reveal the colour of the grain; if you strip them naked the corn will quickly dry. Peel off just one or two layers of onion skin until you get down to one that shines.

Wash potatoes, parsnips, carrots and turnips, but not *too* thoroughly – you do not want them to look as if they have just been tipped out of a supermarket bag. And if the root vegetables are home-grown, keep on the leaves where possible and tie them in bundles, which will look both appetizing and decorative.

As for the container, it would be hard to beat the heavily textured Norfolk rush basket in the photograph. But unless you wish to make that a part of the gift, something that is less of a personal treasure is called for. Plain, straight-sided wooden seed-boxes or round Brie boxes are ideal. Line them with ivy, fig or blackberry foliage or pressed autumn leaves (as described on *page 60*), and they will look superb.

To build up a basket or box of vegetables into even more of a feature, you can add sprays of flowers and dried cereals. Place a piece of soaked foam (partly wrapped in foil) in position and arrange a casual curve of dried wheat, oats and maize seedheads and autumn flowers such as dahlias, chrysanthemums and Chinese lanterns. Then arrange the vegetables in scale with the design, with the largest ones, such as marrows, cauliflowers and cabbages, spilling over on to the floor.

For gifts of small vegetables, you can use cardboard mushroom baskets as conveniently portable containers. Get rid of the jarring shininess of the metal handle by binding it with crêpe or tissue paper, line the basket inside and out and add a layer of leaves that extends over the edges for a natural look.

As a finishing touch to a display of vegetables, add a wisp or two of oats or grasses and a string of luscious black elderberries.

It is very satisfying to arrange different shapes, sizes and colours of vegetables into a still-life group, a glorious centrepiece for the festival of harvest thanksgiving.

AUTUMN SUNSHINE

Pleasing designs can be created, to great effect, with a single flower type. In spring, a tiny posy of gentle violets or primroses; in summer, a vibrant pot of scarlet poppies or bowl of roses; in autumn, a gigantic cauldron of glowing dahlias or chrysanthemums; in winter, a flat dish of floaty Christmas roses or a jug of bright red berries: every season brings a wealth of one-flower, one-pot possibilities.

All bunched up

At harvest festival time, some of the loveliest flower groups you can assemble are with flowers bought inexpensively in unpromising mixed-colour bunches by the roadside or on charity stalls, the produce of enthusiastic gardeners with a prolific cut-flower bed.

Outside a garden gate, a bucket of mixed dahlias produced, very cheaply, the wherewithal for the flower study opposite. First, however, the bunch ties were cut, the stems stripped of all their soggy, slimy leaves, wiped down with a damp cloth, re-cut under water and the flowers plunged deep in a bucket of fresh water.

'Fresh' is the operative word. So often flower-sellers (arrangers too, sometimes) leave on the foliage when they put flowers in water and the lower leaves on branches of foliage. The result is a green and grimy liquid which takes on a smell that becomes increasingly reminiscent of boiled cabbage. The stems drink this in and pass it up to the flowers, which are then expected to thrive.

If flowers are wilting and tired-looking when you buy them, you can often revive them by immersing them completely in cool water, standing them head-first in water once the stems have had a good long drink, or at least spraying them generously with an atomizer, so that they can take up added refreshment – literally – through the petals.

Once these reviving and rejuvenating tactics have been carried out, sort out the flowers quite ruthlessly. Discard any that are crushed, damaged or already shedding their petals as unworthy of further attention. (One dead flower in an arrangement makes the whole display look like a has-been.)

A delight of dahlias

In the group of double and semi-double dahlias *opposite*, planned as a floor-standing arrangement for the harvest festival in a large country church, the container is, somewhat unusually, a huge black cauldron. This dull, matt surface, the product of many a wood fire, is the perfect foil for the brilliance of the flowers, attracting attention to the cream, pink and coral tones. Alternatives might be a large brown earthenware bread crock, an old pudding steamer or saucepan, or even a galvanized bucket. It is surprising what a coat of spray-on matt paint and a few low-trailing leaves can do. Copper, brass or aluminium preserving pans would make specially effective containers for flowers in deeper shades of red and bronze.

The black cauldron was not in perfect condition, so it contains an inner liner, a plastic ice-cream tub. The large aperture is filled with a dome of crushed wire netting, tied round the top with black twine to secure it firmly to the cauldron.

For a full, generous effect, the arrangement is designed like a huge ball. The tallest central stems are positioned first, then all those in graded height, down to the ones that tip the container rim at the front. Although the design is not viewed from the back, flowers are positioned at varying heights, to give balance and avoid the flat-backed 'D' look. All the leaves are glycerined, sprays of lime complete with the delicate flowers, ivy and beech seen to glowing advantage against the shafts of sunlight (*see page 86 for details*).

Ice-cream cone

An alternative way to present flowers-of-a-kind, especially effective when they are viewed from above, is in an ice-cream cone-shape. The stems, all of equal length, are held very close together in the centre and fan out to make a wide V, with the flowers, by now widely spaced, forming a large, flat circle. To do this, you need one or more large, heavy pinholders firmly secured, with florist's water-resistant clay, to the base of a wide, shallow bowl (one from a Victorian wash-stand, for example). If the pinholder is not completely obscured by the stems, scatter a handful of marbles over it.

The matt black surface of this old cauldron allows the brilliant collection of garden dahlias to capture every ray of sunlight – and admiration.

BRIGHT AS A BERRY

Autumn, the season of mellow fruitfulness, offers rich pickings in the gardens and hedgerows, glistening with shiny-bright berries, the luscious fruits and seed-carriers of trees, shrubs and even vegetables. Sprays of these autumn fruits, crimson, scarlet, coral, green, yellow or beautiful black, add an exciting dimension to arrangements of flowers. See how majestically the rowan, hawthorn, cotoneaster and privet berries blend with the group of primarily orange blooms on *page 61*.

Alternatively, they can be a glorious feature in their own right. The small copper measuring-can photographed opposite contains a wealth of hedgerow treasures: a few stems of blackberries with under-ripe fruit at the hard green stage; green holly berries (as yet tough and unappetizing to the birds) and a tight, juicy cluster of the orangey-red seed pods of wild honeysuckle. Now it is the other materials that take second place: purplish-brown sprays of berberis foliage, a small, tightly-closed head of *Helichrysum bracteatum* to match, green umbrellas of hogweed seedheads and long, soft sprays of dock. Together they make an enchantingly simple group for the kitchen dresser.

It is well worth while building up a collection of these colourful materials in autumn. With a quick puff of hair lacquer you can keep the berries in peak condition for several weeks. Deciduous leaves, as they are cut in the autumn, will tumble; often it is best to strip them off and show the berries with evergreen or preserved leaves. Evergreens such as bay, ivy and holly will keep their thrust for a couple of weeks or more. To capture their beauty and undisputed useful-ness forever, preserve evergreen sprays complete with berries with glycerine (*see page 86*). Blackberries shrink very little, lose none of their colour and only a little of their gloss – nothing that hair lacquer cannot restore. The leaves, like preserved rose leaves, deepen to an aubergine colour. Ivy sprays with clusters of berries at either the green or black stage turn a typically chestnut brown. Bay leaves vary from deep apricot to warm, rich brown, and privet turns brownish-black – which then contrasts less effectively with the shiny black berries. Most lovely of all, sprays of variegated holly glycerined with red or yellow berries mellow like ripened fruit: the leaves turn brown and deep gold, sometimes edged with bright red, and the berries deepen in colour. Olive oil, dabbed on with a fine paint-brush, or a puff of lacquer soon restores their sheen.

Variety and versatility

A good collection of plant material (flowers, leaves, seedheads and berries) needs a variety of shapes. Fortu-nately, rose hips (or, more properly, heps) come in such stately shapes and arresting colours that many old-rose fanciers choose their shrubs as much for the magnificence of the autumn fruits as for the summer flowers. Two examples are the sixteenth-century alba Maxima and alba Semi-plena, which both produce large, brilliant heps. The Victorian hybrid sweet-briar rose Anne of Geierstein follows its dark crimson flowers with even more showy scarlet fruits, and *Rosa macro-phylla* produces firm clusters of distinctive bottle-shaped fruits.

Clusters of the bright scarlet or orange rowanberries are held on much less rigid stems, and therefore need careful placing.

All the Sorbus tree family are good berry-makers. There are the golden brown fruits of the hybridized whitebeam, Wilfred Fox; the golden yellow clusters adorning trees of the Joseph Rock variety throughout the winter and the *Sorbus domestica*, the service tree, with its green and red-tinged pear-shaped fruits.

Hawthorn berries span the colour wheel from dark brick-red to light and bright coral, which has stronger impact. Cotoneaster has stunning flat clusters of brilliant orange berries that far outshine its modest white flowers and if nesting sparrows have not eaten them all will make wonderful Christmas decorations.

Do not forget the vegetable garden. Asparagus pro-duces beautiful large, round orange fruits on every side-shoot. Gently strip off the now-brittle fern 'leaves' and cut off some of the lowest shoots, thick with berries, to use separately. Otherwise the whole plant, a tree in miniature, is somewhat unwieldy.

Mingle some jet-black berries with these showpieces for maximum effect: for example, elderberries, shown on *page 63*, privet (*page 61*) and ivy.

A small group of plant material is a welcome addition to the hurly-burly of a busy kitchen. The copper measuring-jug holds shiny-bright sprays of blackberries, at the attractive pale green stage.

67

CHRISTENING PARTY

Flowers for a christening should perhaps aim for simplicity. Just like weddings, baptisms are celebrated in two separate locations, the church and the home, and both will be greatly enhanced by arrangements of seasonal flowers. But large formal displays are not usually called for.

As always when planning flowers to decorate a church, it is important to discuss your ideas with the priest. Tell him whether your plans include decorating the font, the centre of attention at a baptism, for some priests eschew any adornment whatever of this holy symbol. If you are unsure, ask him to show you just where the baptismal party will stand, so that you can best judge where any free-standing flower arrangements will be most admired and least in the way.

The advice on *page 40* about measuring up might be helpful on this occasion too. Try to ensure that your designs reflect the character of the building and make the most of its decorative features.

It is always pleasant to welcome guests arriving at a church with a display of flowers just inside the door. As an alternative to a conventional pedestal arrangement, you could place a large basket of flowers on a wooden or metal stand. The design on *page 71* could be adapted for such use. For greater impact, include a few larger flowers, perhaps fully-open roses and carnations, with longer tendrils of foliage so that basket and pedestal are visually knitted together by the plant materials. A pair of basket-pedestals on each side of the font, a basket spilling over with trailing flowers and leaves on a flight of steps – each church will suggest its own locations.

Decorating the font

The type and style of the font, too, will influence the decorations. Usually there is a ledge around the top rim where, with the necessary permission, you can arrange a circlet of flowers. Remember that these must in no way be fussy or intrusive; their role is to adorn the ceremony, not to interfere with it. A straight ledge around the pedestal base could also hold a flower ring.

The posy ring on *page 15* would adapt beautifully for a font; it is garnished with pink-for-a-girl and blue-for-a-boy flowers, and the colour balance could be altered as appropriate. To create the design around a font, protect the surface with a hoop of plastic or foil, measured and cut exactly to fit, and cover it with blocks of soaked plastic foam. Then work the design just as described, adding flowers and leaves so that all foam and protective base material are out of sight. Add long trails of, for example, variegated ivy, periwinkle, lamium, honeysuckle or clematis at intervals, and tuck a few tiny flowers – spray pinks, marguerites, cornflowers – among the leaves.

If the font has a wide, cylindrical pedestal, a spiral of leaves and flowers twining around it can be most effective. A ribbon of flowers like this is simple, though somewhat time-consuming, to make. Take a piece of thick string or cord, sticky-tape it to the top of the pillar and wind it round and round to the base to gauge the length of 'ribbon' needed. Cut a basket of evergreen foliage such as ivy, lime-green or silver-grey cupressus (the dark greens can look depressing), eucalyptus or laurel, or use the florists' standby, the soft, fluffy, frondy trails of *Asparagus sparenduli*. Make up small bunches of foliage and wire them close together all along the string – fuse wire is easy to use and unobtrusive. Long trails of ivy or the asparagus can be wired on without bunching, then reinforced with more leaves to cover any gaps. Then wire on flowers to match your other arrangements – single spray chrysanthemums, sprays of orange blossom, bunches of thrift or whatever. Fix the flower ribbon to the top and base of the pillar with something like blue tacky-clay, which will not leave marks.

A flower ribbon, or swag, can be used to great effect to decorate the front of the tablecloth on a buffet-table or the one displaying the cake. Measure the length needed, looping from each corner and up to the table-top in the centre and work it as described. Fix the swag to the cloth with pins or stitches.

Sometimes the simplest designs are the prettiest. For a summer christening party (opposite) each small table was decorated with a small vase of sweet peas, and the parents' table had a symbolic, though optimistic, extra – a little angel!

On some occasions – and the baptism of a child is certainly one – simple flower groups have a particular charm. A delicate Victorian vase is a lovely foil for sweet peas.

CENTRE OF ATTRACTION

A basket of flowers is a beautiful centrepiece for the table at a christening party, combining both the joy and the simplicity of the occasion. Depending on size and shape, the basket could form a very acceptable part of a christening gift with a practical life ever after, holding all the bits and bobs needed for the care of the baby.

Some of the prettiest baskets around, wide, deep and with a semicircular handle, are woven from natural willow and sprayed with matt paint in pale tints. They retain the thick, rough and characteristic texture of the craft, but offer a choice of colours to tone with furnishings and fabrics. Pink, blue, deep cream or mint green, the most popular colours, would all be lovely on this occasion.

For the long hoop-handled basket in our photograph, we chose a soft silver-grey matt paint, from a range of aerosol cans, and sprayed the basket inside and out with two coats.

Flowers for the baby

Some flowers seem instinctively more 'right' for a christening than others. Basically, dark, deep colours and large, heavy blooms are out of court and should on this occasion give way to the loveliest of flowers in clear or delicate tones. For the christening of a baby girl flowers in several shades of pink should, to avoid monotony, be blended with white, cream or pale coral. For the same reason, blue flowers for a boy should be mingled with mauve, perhaps some pink, white, cream or pale lemon. Otherwise, to get away from the colour tradition entirely, nothing could be prettier, for either sex, than a basket of milky-white parchment and pale yellow flowers ribboned with trails of pale cream and green variegated foliage.

In the springtime there is plenty of choice among the soft-coloured daffodils, narcissi and tulips. If friends offer you the run of their gardens for the occasion you might be lucky enough to come across white daffodils with lovely pink trumpets (Salome is a pretty example); orchid-flowered or double white narcissi; double peony-flowered tulips, their petals opened out almost flat, or parrot tulips with their frilled and cut petal edges. All are a far cry from the bright reds and yellows usually associated with these bulbs.

Snowdrops, violets and primroses, redolent of childhood, are all delightful for christening decoration. Bunches or posies of violets can be used as the 'rounds' intermingled with cream and white flowers, specially suitable in designs for infant boys.

Roses, carnations, pinks, peonies, azaleas, rhododendrons, lilies, mallow, alstroemeria, Californian poppies, sweet peas, love-in-a-mist, asters, clarkia, scabious, cornflowers, godetia, cosmos, the summer selection of flowers is many and various. As autumn comes, consider pale pink geraniums and pelargoniums, the ubiquitous single and double spray chrysanthemums, clary, michaelmas daisies, the more modest of the dahlias (in both size and colour), and the last roses of summer.

Winter flower arrangements bring together the last of the autumn and the first of the spring flowers – happily arriving in the markets earlier every year. Hellebores, Christmas roses, winter jasmine and anemones have great potential. If stocks really flag, you can mix and mingle a few dried immortelles with fresh flowers. The pale pink and white helipterum, white *Ammobium alatum* and the palest colours of the mixed *Helichrysum bracteatum* would all be suitable.

Filling the basket

The silver basket opposite holds a dainty collection of summer flowers, pink and cream roses, cream double carnations tinged with deep pink (linking the colours in the scheme), spray pinks and cream single spray chrysanthemums.

First of all, the handle is bound with trails of ivy leaves. A large block of soaked stem-holding foam is stood on end, in a container to protect the table, and extends well above the rim of the basket.

The flowers are positioned to form a gentle curve from the topmost pink rose to the lowest bud, and then the basket is filled in, shape alternating with shape, colour with colour. Lastly, long trails and short sprays of foliage are added – lamium, ivy and snippings of carnation.

A silver-sprayed basket, the handle twined with ivy, is filled with pink and cream carnations, pinks and spray chrysanthemums to make an eye-catching table centrepiece.

BLUE FOR A BOY

When designing flowers for the christening of a son it is not just a matter of substituting blue cornflowers for the old-fashioned pinks and sprays of Oxford blue larkspur for the pink clarkia: a different approach entirely is needed.

Start with the container. Blue and white china seems made for the job. You could create a tall, upright design for the table centre, balanced a-top a slender Oriental vase, as here. It is simple, effective, unfussy and forthright. A blue and white Chinese ginger jar (like the one visible in the background) could hold a full, free arrangement of hyacinths, double cream narcissi and cream and blue anemones or, later in the year, blue and yellow Californian poppies, blue Iberian cranesbill, white campion and gypsophila. Later still it could blossom with an autumn study of blue salvia, centaurea, white Japanese anemones and fluffy clusters of white pearl everlasting.

Teapots and coffee pots, whether precious family heirlooms or part of an up-to-the-minute set, are reassuringly easy to use as containers and not too delicate or dainty for an infant son's celebration. *Pages 20–21*, where a pink and white teapot holds a display of spring flowers, and *pages 54–5*, with a rose-filled coffee-pot, show the sorts of effect that can be achieved. If your choice is for the distinctively soft Wedgwood blue ware, take care with the exact shades of blue and mauve you include.

Blue and white plates could act as platforms for lovely table designs (an unusual one, an early hotplate, appears in the photograph opposite). Stick a foam pinholder to one side, press a block of foam into the spikes and make an arrangement in a gentle, flowing curve or a lazy L-shape; it is much like making an arrangement on a tray. For the long points you could use white stocks or broom and blue larkspur, white roses for the rounds, and leafy sprays of forget-me-nots and lime-green alchemilla mollis as the fillers.

If the blue and white container is very heavily patterned, like for example, the classic willow pattern, minimize the use of blue in the plant material. Cream or white and pale yellow with just touches of blue alkanet or borage would be cleaner and less confusing.

Instead of a blue and white container you could of course choose either blue or white. Choose plain white when there is an abundance of blue flowers to select from, blue containers when they are few and far between.

Turning flowers blue

You can even cheat by colouring flowers a pale shade of blue, simply by standing them in ink. Then you can have carnations, spray carnations, single spray and double chrysanthemums and other unlikely blooms such as arum lilies all proclaiming 'blue for a boy'.

Make a solution of one part dark blue ink to two parts water. Stand the flower stems in it and leave them for an hour or two to turn blue. This only works with fairly sturdy flowers, but the general principle opens up many possibilities. (Yes, it works with other colours, too, of course, but blue is notoriously the most difficult one to find in all the shapes and sizes you are likely to need.)

Tall and stately

The tall, upright arrangement opposite was designed around the urn-shaped Oriental vase. It is an example of how to use a strongly-patterned container with flowers in two contrasting colours from that pattern without the whole effect being jumbled. The cream spider chrysanthemums form a ring round the cluster of bluebells and grape hyacinths in the centre. The speckled lily leaf, placed vertically, emphasizes the nature of the design and becomes the focal point.

A purpose-made plastic saucer fitted with a cylinder of soaked foam is stuck to the neck of the vase with OasisFix and, for extra security, water-resistant tape.

The fan-shape of arum lily leaves is positioned first, then the chrysanthemum buds at the back that define the height. The blue flowers are placed next, close together in a tight bunch, followed by the large, showy, spidery flowers facing forward and to each side.

The arum lily leaves need special care to prevent them wilting. Singe the stem ends as soon as they are cut, then immerse them in a bowl of water.

A blue and white slender vase, a good choice
for the christening of a baby boy, holds
bluebells, grape hyacinths and cream spider
chrysanthemums arranged among
arum lily leaves.

LASTING MEMENTOES

As the year passes and so many of the garden and wild flowers become just a lovely memory, it is time to think of stocking up for the winter with preserved flowers, grasses, seedheads and leaves.

By the same methods you can preserve flowers from special celebrations or family occasions, to treasure as lasting mementoes: for a bride, perhaps the scented stocks from the church decorations; for a longer-married woman, the heather from an anniversary bouquet; for a mother, a posy of rosebuds from the christening.

Many plant materials can be dried until they are crisp and papery – and then virtually everlasting – simply by being hung in a dry, airy room, or standing in loose bunches in wide-necked containers. A free circulation of warm, dry air draws out the natural moisture from the plant; without this moisture bacteria cannot develop and the petals and seedheads will not deteriorate. What is more, they will retain practically all their original colour and shape.

For single, composite and trumpet-shaped flowers, drying in desiccants (*see pages 87–8*) works best.

Everlasting flowers

A whole kaleidoscope of colourful flowers which have the convenient characteristic of drying naturally on the plants: these are the 'everlastings', also known as immortelles. Among them are the long-stemmed, closely-clustered flowers of statice *Limonium sinuatum*, which you can grow or buy in almost any colour: sharp lemon yellow, gold, salmon, peach, pink, purple, mauve, blue or white, or almost any combination of those hues. There are bunches of statice hanging on the left in the photograph opposite. Along the top row is a close relation, wild sea lavender, which, with its minute white flowers on silvery-grey stems, makes a good neutral filler. Mingling with the sea lavender is a material of similar colouring but contrasting shape: white pearl everlasting, the tiny round white flowers blending beautifully with more colourful subjects.

Among the most colourful of everlasting subjects are the strawflowers, *Helichrysum bracteatum*, the round, daisy-shaped flowers on the top left. These grow in all the sunshine shades of red, purple, orange, gold, yellow and cream and will 'lift' any flower group. In winter you can arrange a few strawflowers with evergreen or preserved leaves for a bright and long-lasting design; towards Christmas, add a few berries.

All the other daisy-shaped or composite everlastings are much more low-key in colour. Pink or white helipterum, small single, flat daisies with bright yellow centres, are the most romantic of dried flowers – ideal for a long-enduring Valentine posy or anniversary gift. By contrast, white winged everlastings, also known as *Ammobium alatum grandiflorum*, are much more robust, double daisy flowers with thick, domed yellow centres.

Not technically 'everlasting' or even flowers, but just as useful to the flower-arranger, are Chinese lanterns, the bright orange bunches hanging on the right of the photograph. These brilliantly coloured seedpods dry on the plant, the leaves drop off and you are left with instant winter decorations. For less vigorous colour, you can hang bunches of the lanterns in strong light or sunlight and they will fade, gradually, to mellow parchment. They are shown at various stages of sun-bleaching in the autumn array on *page 77*, and in an 'alternative Christmas tree' design on *page 83*.

As bright light draws the colour from dried or preserved plant materials, always store them in a dark room, such as an attic or loft, or at least a shady corner – unless you want to bleach them, of course.

Grasses and all the cereals – wheat, oats, wild oats, barley and rye – with their delicate cream colouring combine well with both fresh and dried flowers and are especially appropriate for harvest thanksgiving designs. Quaking grass (*Briza maxima*) and hare's-tail grass (*Lagurus ovatus*), the prettiest of the decorative grasses, are used to good effect in a lasting memento of cream, brown and lemon on *page 79*.

As with grasses, so with seedheads; it is the shape, not necessarily the colour, that distinguishes them. The purplish-blue urns that launch a thousand poppy seeds; the vividly striped pods of love-in-a-mist criss-crossed with lace-like tendrils; the stems of velvety lupin pods, like furry rabbits' ears; the little chestnut brown nut-shapes of rue seedheads and the flower-like pods of Greek spiny spurge – these are some examples.

Bunches of flowers, everlastings, seedheads and grasses hanging in an old barn to dry are pretty as a picture in the process, and are delightful 'raw materials' for year-round arrangements.

GOLDEN TONES

If you have ever looked lingeringly at a crop of flowers and wished they could last for ever, remember that a great many garden and wild flowers can be preserved by the simple air-drying method.

The most successful candidates for drying in this way are all the plants composed of a mass of tiny flowers or florets formed into clusters. Examples are the umbrella-shaped flowers, known as umbellifers, like yarrow, achillea and tansy; the spherical forms like allium, chives and garlic, and the long spikes of flowers, so useful for the 'points' in a design, clarkia, lavender, larkspur and *Statice suworowii*. These give consistently better results than single, separate flowers, because if the flowers are in tightly-packed clusters the slight loss of size and form that takes place as the moisture evaporates is barely discernible.

Harvest time

Gather flowers, grasses and seedheads for drying on a dry, warm day, after the morning dew has disappeared and before the evening mist settles. Watch each clump of flowers carefully and harvest them when they are just at their peak for preserving: in most cases, just before they are fully opened, though statice, one of the everlastings, is an exception, and should be left to mature and dry on the plant. Cut the long spires of delphinium, golden rod and clarkia when some of the lower flowers are fully out and the buds at the top are still firmly closed. At this stage they not only dry most satisfactorily, but, tapering to a point, are most attractive for arranging.

A treasure hunt in the garden or countryside should provide some pretty seedheads to dry. In addition to those mentioned on *page 78* there are the star-shaped pods of mallow to use in miniature designs, like tiny silver flowers, the brown tulip-shaped pods of aquilegia, the large, almost rectangular pods of some lilies (very effective at Christmas-time sprayed silver, gold or red) and the spiky egg-shaped teasels that are so much more familiar than the plant's minute mauve flowers.

Gather the pods after the seeds have scattered naturally, or, if you want to save the seed yourself, cut the stems just before the pods burst, tie a paper bag over the seedheads and hang them in bunches.

Cut the stems of all plant materials as long as possible and strip off all the leaves, which would just dry into a mess. Hang or stand all materials in a warm, dry atmosphere. Leave them until they are papery-dry – anything from one to three weeks – and then store them, still hanging in bunches, standing in containers or loosely packed in boxes in a warm, dry room. Never store dried materials in a damp shed or garage. There they will re-absorb moisture, and start to decay.

Large stems such as delphiniums benefit from a quicker burst of heat and give better results, hung singly or at the most in twos or threes, in an airing cupboard or over the boiler, where they will dry in three to four days. You can also dry tight little rosebuds in this way, tied in bunches and hanging upside down. Though pretty, the results will not be perfect.

Arranging dried materials

Once dried, flowers and seedheads are very light indeed – virtually weightless – and can be wilful. You press a stem into a piece of dry foam, reach for the next and find the first one has sprung out again. This is why you should leave the stems long, so that there is plenty to press deep into the foam or container. There is a special greyish-brown stem-holding foam for dried materials that grips them firmly. Without this and in an emergency you can use dry the green foam that is sold for use with fresh flowers, but it does not provide such firm anchorage and is inclined to break up.

The design opposite had too many stems to crowd into the neck of the mustard jar, so a plastic foam-holding saucer was stuck on top, with a cylinder of the grey foam pressed into it. The love-in-a-mist seedheads and the oats and wheat that point out the triangle were placed first, then, stage by stage, the shape was filled in, with Chinese lanterns in all shades of orange, bright lemon yellow statice, large round pale green seedheads of Jerusalem sage, tiny white daisy-like helipterum, clusters of golden yellow *Helichrysum siculum*, another everlasting, large gold umbrellas of tansy, clusters of orange dyed pearl everlasting and, trailing over the jar, monochromatic sprays of sea lavender.

All the design will need in the next few months is a gentle breeze from a hairdryer to blow off the dust.

Lovely colour mixtures derive from a collection of dried-flower materials. This one contains oats, wheat, love-in-a-mist and Jerusalem sage seedheads, everlastings, golden tansy and orange Chinese lanterns.

MAGIC IN MINIATURE

Two large, unruly bushes of rue tumbling over a garden pathway; a windswept verge by a busy main road; a clump of barbed-wire-like Greek spiny spurge clinging to a barren hillside; a patch of delicate, decorative grasses blowing in the breeze; a little square of herb garden outside a kitchen window, and a strip of everlasting flowers growing in a stony corner – these were the starting points for the dried-flower arrangement opposite.

The size of growing plants has no relation to the way they are used once the flowers or seedheads are dried – one reason why dried-flower collecting and arranging is so fascinating. The tiny seedpods of common rue and fringed rue, insignificant on the bush, are like nuts in miniature silhouetted at the edges of our design. Waist-high stems of bladder campion are as nothing by the roadside after the dainty white petals have blown – until, after air-drying, a few snippings show up like translucent urns in the metal cream-churn. Risk lacerations and abrasions cutting the seedheads from huge, unfriendly boulders of spiny spurge and you are rewarded with a handful of pale beige already-dried 'flowers' as dainty as any daisies.

Long stems of lupins with the grey furry pods carried in twos can be snipped down to make small elements, each pair of seedpods like silvery wings. Tall, stately spires of golden rod, which dry perfectly, yield rich pickings of small, pencil-long side shoots, perfect for establishing the boundaries of small-scale designs. Even long columns of dried delphinium produce carbon copies of themselves many times smaller in their side shoots.

Think small

You can use dried materials to make pretty posies that last for almost a lifetime, a charmingly romantic gift made all the more so: in the traditional language of flowers, not surprisingly, all everlastings signify memory, and never-ceasing remembrance.

To make a dried flower posy follow the general principles outlined on *page 18*. Select a central feature, a tiny rosebud, a small bunch of lavender or a cluster of pearl everlasting and hold it in one hand. Encircle that with clippings of statice or tiny seedheads; then make another circle, and another, contrasting shapes and colours. Enfold the posy in preserved leaves – glycerined beech, ivy or oak, for instance, and bind the stems with twine. Tie it round and make a narrow bow of satin ribbon with long trails.

Very small baskets with handles are perfect containers for little nosegays of dried flowers, and make the prettiest Christmas tree decorations. Put a small block of dried foam in each basket, push a wire through to secure it to the base, and tuck the wire away. Arrange in them a selection of colourful flowers – helichrysum buds, sprays of statice, clippings of clarkia and larkspur, with alchemilla mollis and gypsophila for fillers: result – decorative little hanging baskets you can store for years.

Small arrangements of dried flowers are invaluable for table decorations. You could make one for each table-setting at a dinner party. Use small wine-glasses, coffee cups, eggcups – slightly damaged ones will do – herb and spice jars or even the side-tapering golden cap of a whisky bottle. Cut a wedge of dry grey foam to fit the neck and, for maximum flexibility, extend just above it so you can angle stems downwards.

Use your dried materials – and imagination – to create individual designs combining preserved leaves, flowers and seedheads, remembering that many leaves, too, can be separated into small leaflets for work on this scale. When you are arranging dried flowers, never throw anything away. Every snipping from a large stem, every stray leaflet, floret and straggly bud has the makings of magic in miniature.

The cream churn

The small metal cream churn shown opposite is a distinctive container: a brass or copper measure, small jug or glass storage jar would be just as suitable. The holding material is a block of grey foam wedged into and protruding over the rim. The design is built up from the back downwards, with preserved sage leaves providing visual weight at the base and perfectly complementing the grey metal.

Small brown seedheads, like tiny nuts or carved wooden flowers, contrast delightfully with snippings of grasses, spiny spurge, grey furry lupin seedpods and zingy lemon-yellow everlastings.

12 DAYS OF CHRISTMAS

Amid the hurly-burly of the Christmas preparations, the time I treasure most is spent wandering into the garden and down the lane with a trug and secateurs, gathering greenery.

From our hedge I cut thick clusters of mid-green ivy on woody stems, each one chosen for its cluster of pale green or black berries – surely as striking as any winter flower. For special emphasis or a design lacking highlights, spray the berries red, gold or silver, or just splattered with touches of white. To do this, and to keep the paint off the leaves, cut a slit in a piece of card and slip this over the berry stem.

Some apple trees on the corner are entwined with two other kinds of ivy, one with long trails of small dark green foliage and the other with larger, variegated leaves. These are both useful for long vertical designs: I make a leafy swag to outline the fireplace and an archway, and the 'stick camouflage' in the 'fruit tree' (*see overleaf*), for example. Large ivy leaves are specially good at hiding the stem-holding materials in flower arrangements – foam, wire, pinholders and so forth.

Beside the garden gate there is a huge tapering cypress tree in a deep shade of blue. A few short sprays from this contrast well with rather more cuttings from a lime-green variety near the fishpond. These fan-shaped sprays make a very good basis, bound first on to the string, for evergreen swags or the wire hoop for door wreaths.

A stone's throw from our garden gate stands a huge holly tree that is usually thick with berries. Each December we watch, agonized, as the birds zoom in and out, emerging with juice round their beaks. If they appear to be stripping the tree too soon, I cut some branches ahead of schedule and give them the usual treatment for woody stems. Scrape off an inch or so of the bark, split the stem ends, and strip off the lower leaves (wearing gardening gloves). Stand the stems deep in water and spray them every day or so with the fine rose on the watering-can. I have known holly stay fresh-looking in the garage for over a month, and then last well indoors after that.

Further down the lane there is a freak holly tree, an absolute boon for evergreen arrangements, although it is actually yellow. The leaves always 'fade' to a brilliant lemon-marmalade colour and a few snippings of this are worth their weight in gold.

Down by the farm gate there is a very tall spindle tree that comes into all its pinky-red glory just in time for Christmas. A few stems of this mingle cheerfully with any of the greens, as in the candle ring on *page 85*, for example, and can give you a Christmas colour theme with a difference: matching pink candles instead of traditional red.

A patch of brambles in winter can yield some gorgeous plum and purple-coloured leaves, very pretty arranged with a few precious flowers, especially pink tones, and mingled with both dark and pale greens.

On the circular route back home a neighbour has a lovely blue spruce tree overhanging the lane, each branch looking as if it has just been touched with frost, a perfect colour combination.

It is surprising how productive any garden can be, even at this time of year: there are usually a few rose leaves worth cutting; perhaps a few stems of rue, stachys or santolina; some side branches you can spare from evergreen shrubs like azalea, rhododendron and camellia; light yellowy-green shoots and long trails of periwinkle or variegated lamium, always faintly glistened with white on the deep green leaves; eucalyptus is another possibility.

Sometimes other treasures are found: skeletonized holly or laurel leaves beneath the bushes, all the fleshy tissues worn and washed away to leave just the dainty network of veins – perfect partners with dried flowers or small fresh blooms. Chinese lanterns do this, too: I always leave some stems in the garden in hope.

Jug of berries

The bright and cheerful arrangement opposite was achieved with the minimum of materials, and of time. The leaves, complementing each other in both colour and shape, are cupressus, silvery-grey, furry ballota, ivy and holly, with a few long stems of zingy-red rose hips. As for the holly berries, this was one year when the birds almost won and about half are fake, bought in bunches and twisted on to the stems.

Choose evergreen leaves that contrast
strikingly with each other – shiny-bright and
dark green holly and ivy, matt and greyish-
green cupressus and ballota – and
you need only a few choice berries.

VARIATIONS ON A THEME

Ladies and gentlemen, as a celebration of this most joyful time of year, and to decorate your homes in the most unusual fashion, we proudly present the alternative Christmas tree. Our trees take up less room than the traditional Norway spruce, they do not need decking out with frills, furbelows and fancy gifts, they do not shed needles on the carpet, and they are child's play (though a little time-consuming) to make. Gather round for full details.

The tree in the centre clings closest to tradition. As you can see, it is a fruit tree, laden with apples and satsumas, heavy with rose hips, and a great delight to the birds. The evergreen leaves are cupressus and laurel, which will last for the twelve days of Christmas and more.

The other two trees are composed entirely of dried flowers, seedpods and nuts, the ultimate in decorative ways to use headless flowers, single 'lanterns' and tiny sprays from your snippings box. On the left is the strawflower tree, a colourful riot of *Helichrysum bracteatum* flowers, interspersed with sprays of pearl, statice and other everlasting flowers and, as highlights, Chinese lanterns.

On the right is the dried orange tree, a more modest-hued species, blossoming with papery-brown honesty seedpods and the silvery 'moons' left when the seeds have blown, poppy seedheads from pale grey to deep mauve, chestnuts and acorns in their rich brown tones, *Helichrysum bracteatum*, strawflowers (this time in only lemon and pale orange colours), *Helichrysum siculum* in palest lemon, Chinese lanterns sun-bleached to modest shades of orange, white pearl everlasting and, finally, sprays of this most useful of fillers dyed burnt sienna.

All the trees, round balls of colour, burgeon from the top of 120-cm (4-foot) canes planted in 22.5-cm (9-inch)-wide clay flower-pots. The fruit tree grows out of a ball of crumpled chicken wire, and the strawflower and dried orange trees are created on large squashed-flat paper lampshades (for instructions *see page 88*). There are few tricks of the trade to know about: it is more a question of making up your mind in good time and getting the whole family enthusiastic.

The fruit tree, as elegant and stylish as a clipped green bay tree, looks marvellous in a porch and is completely weather-resistant. Rain will not damage the tree – on the contrary, it will freshen it up; snow would surely enhance it, but wind is a menace. If the tree is vulnerable, as in an open porch, tie it to a post.

Stand our prolific evergreen tree in the centre of a window, or make it the focal point of a room corner, with Christmas parcels piled high around the base. This tree, with its shiny laurel leaves and the light golden cupressus, positively sparkles with the addition of a string of fairy lights. Choose the tiny pinhead kind; they look specially pretty in a single colour, such as yellow, or red, or orange.

The strawflower tree and the dried orange tree are very definitely indoor standards. If space permits, one just inside the front door will provide an instant talking point for visitors. These trees would also look fabulous in an alcove, an archway or a well-lit corner.

Table-top trees

You can easily make miniature copies of these floor-standing trees as table decorations. Both the evergreen 'fruit' tree and the dried-flower trees would be lovely table centrepieces for The Meal itself. A pair of small trees could stand at each end of a sideboard, mantlepiece or long buffet-table.

Follow the general instructions on *page 88*. For the table-top versions of all three designs, anchor a 30-cm (12-inch) cane in a 10-cm (4-inch) flower-pot. Push a 7-cm (2½-inch)-diameter ball of stem-holding foam on the top. You can buy these from florists; use the green foam, soaked in water for evergreens, and the 'dried flower' grey foam for the others.

For the evergreen fruit tree, use small snippings of holly, ivy, cupressus, privet, camellia, yew or whatever is available. 'Real' fruit will make a small tree top-heavy; instead, push in stems of rose hips, clusters of red or yellow holly berries, preserved berries from your collection or the pink fruits of the spindle tree.

You will need dried materials on short stems for your table-top trees. Be sure to keep the shape round, not ragged, and fill in any gaps with clippings of small everlastings. Ribbon bows are the final flourish.

Tradition takes a tumble with these
'alternative' Christmas trees, two made with
dried flowers and seedheads and the third
with sprays of evergreens, apples
and clementines.

CANDLE RING

In celebration of Christmas a colourful candle ring, a hoop of mixed evergreens, tree-berry fruits and flickering flames, makes a beautiful, long-lasting centrepiece for the table or, as we have photographed it opposite, a free-standing decoration, standing on a red, upturned waste-paper bin. In this way, it evokes the spirit of the traditional Christmas tree, glowing with candles in tiny holders at the tips of the branches.

The visual impact of the candle ring is in direct proportion to the variety of evergreens you can find. The holly and the ivy are always effective seasonal decorations, but how much more so when they are variegated! Go for a good contrast of grey-blue and greeny-yellow colours; of blue spruce, Japanese cedar or rue with the sunnier tones of variegated holly, periwinkle or eleagnus, lime-green cupressus or golden privet. Contrast matt and shiny finishes, the furry-leaved ballota, stachys or senecio with laurel, camellia or rhododendron, and smooth and spiky textures, yew, juniper and pine with sprays of ivy or bay.

If you do not have the pick of a garden or a neighbouring hedgerow, a bunch of holly and a spray of mistletoe from the market, with a couple of clippings from an indoor ivy, will give you a pretty good start.

Holly, mistletoe and other berries, the green or black seed-clusters of ivy and the pinky-red sprays of spindle fruits would all add greatly to the interest. So do cones. Wrap a florist's stub wire round the base of small cones and push them into the foam.

Foundations

The candle ring is based on a custom-made plastic hoop about 25 cm (10 inches) in diameter, available from florists. It is 6 cm (2¼ inches) across and 5 cm (2 inches) deep, a round channel ready to fill with small blocks and off-cuts of soaked stem-holding foam, and then with leaves, or with flowers (the same base can be seen in its summer guise in the posy ring on *page 15*). As an alternative, you can use a wire hoop frame, the kind sold for door wreaths. Cover the top and bottom with clumps of moss, then fit small blocks of foam around the top, wired over and round with a roll of fuse wire. It works, but it takes more time and effort.

Position the candles first, one for each day of the festival, then fill in with sprays of evergreens, berries and nuts. Freshen up the design from time to time with a fine shower of water from an atomizer.

Suspensions

If you opt for the wire-hoop type of base, you can turn the design into a hanging decoration. This links with the old tradition of hanging circlets of holly and ivy, adorned with apples, over the banqueting table. In this case, cover both the tops and base of the hoop with moss and thin blocks of foam. Position stems of contrasting evergreens to cover it entirely on all sides.

To fix on apples – the smallest and rosiest you can find – push a florist's stub wire horizontally through the top, bend back the short end and twist-tie it to the long end. Loop the long end of wire under a wire on the hoop and twist-tie it in place. Tie red or orange ribbon bows to conceal the wire near the apple stalks. Suspend the apple ring with four lengths of thick ribbon evenly spaced so that it hangs level. For a truly medieval touch spray the apples gold, known as 'endoring', before adding them to the decoration. Add a few short bursts of gold spray-paint to the evergreens, too, so that they look as if they have been lightly spattered by a shower of golden rain.

Taking the circle of evergreens and fruit notion one stage further, you can pretty-up a door wreath with small apples, satsumas or pears. A hoop of golden cupressus, variegated holly and deep green ivy looks stunning with wired-on fruit instead of berries or flowers. Wire the fruit as described, position each piece close against the evergreens so that it nestles among the leaves, and wire it to the hoop. A bunch of three or five small apples or pears hanging from the top and into the centre of the hoop is effective.

One word of warning: it is probably a good idea to include as many prickly evergreens as possible; the more holly the merrier. The last time I adorned my door wreath with Cox's orange pippins I was treated to the endearing sight of a field mouse sitting a-top the decoration and munching his way through a tasty Christmas dinner.

A lovely idea for the table centre – or
to hang above the festive table: a ring of
evergreen leaves decorated with a bright red
candle for each of the twelve days
of Christmas.

PRACTICAL TIPS

Preserving foliage

Sprays of preserved foliage and dramatic single leaves are a delightful accompaniment to arrangements of both fresh and dried flowers. At times when supplies of garden foliage are reduced to the faithful evergreens, and the florists offer Hobson's choice of one or two all-too-familiar kinds, it is wonderful to have a collection of supple, mellow and russety sprays at your disposal.

Once they are preserved, many leaves take on the characteristics of autumn foliage. Silver birch – which you can preserve complete with catkins on the twigs – are transformed, turning all shades from yellow to deep brown; preserved maple, most spectacular of leaves, ranges from very light cream to very dark chestnut brown; oak and beech turn to a warm mid-brown; eucalyptus leaves become deep cream, and blackberry – which you can treat with the berries *in situ* – turn reddish-brown, still tinged with silver on the reverse.

You can treat evergreen leaves such as blackberry, bay, laurel, holly, ivy and cupressus at any time of year, and indeed it is useful to have fresh and preserved supplies side by side. Preserved bay becomes orangey brown and contrasts well with the fresh deep green sprays; laurel goes almost jet and shiny black; holly varies from mid to deep tones of brown and looks very rich; ivy goes such a deep brown it can look almost black; and cupressus, which you can treat in fan-shaped sprays complete with cones, goes a deep honey gold.

There is a deadline on preserving all deciduous leaves: you must cut and treat them by midsummer, when the sap is still rising in the plant and the leaves are absorbing moisture. Do not try to capture them too soon, for very young and tender leaves will only wilt under the strain.

Be discriminating about the leaves you select. Basically only perfect specimens are worth the time and trouble. Strip off all lower leaves and discard any that are insect- or weather-damaged. Strip off the bark from the ends of all woody stems for about 5 cm (2 inches). Very lightly crush the stem ends, using a wooden rolling-pin or tent-peg mallet, for example, or split them twice, criss-cross, with a very sharp knife.

This will enable the stems to take up the preserving solution more readily.

The glycerine solution Mix a solution of one part glycerine with two parts of very hot water, bring it to the boil, stirring, then leave it to cool slightly. Pour the solution into a heatproof container to a depth of about 5 cm (2 inches). Old toughened glass or earthenware preserving jars, vases or, for large sprays, buckets are suitable.

Stand the stems in the hot preserving solution, making sure they are pushed down well into the liquid. Leave them in a cool place, away from direct light, until the foliage has absorbed the moisture; globules of the liquid will appear on the leaves.

The process time will depend on the thickness of the leaves and the stage at which they were cut. Beech leaves are usually ready within 4–7 days, sycamore take 1½–2 weeks, blackberry, hellebores and holly take 3 weeks and sprays of fig leaves can need 6–7 weeks to become supple and fully treated.

But there is a short-cut you can take with large, thick leaves such as fig, bergenia and fatsia japonica. Cut them from the stems and preserve them, two or three at a time, completely immersed in a shallow dish of the glycerine solution. That way you cut the process time to 1–2 weeks for fig and 2–3 weeks for fatsia japonica.

When the leaves (both sprays and 'singles') are ready, remove them from the solution and wipe the leaves and stems with a dry cloth. If you wish to use the sprays with fresh flowers, in water, spray or paint the stems with a water-resistant varnish. Wire single leaves on to florist's wires and, for a neat appearance, bind the wires with green or brown florist's water-resistant tape, or gutta percha.

A skeleton of their former selves

Nature sometimes plays a decorative trick on evergreen leaves and strips them of all the green plant tissue, leaving just the finely veined structure, or 'skeleton'. You can often find skeletonized bay, holly, ivy, magnolia or laurel leaves under trees or bushes, and you can buy skeletonized magnolia leaves, sometimes bleached or dyed, in florists' shops and at floral art clubs.

These lace-like leaves are particularly attractive with dried flowers, to frame a posy or spray of fresh spring or summer flowers, or to mingle with evergreens, the perfect contrast, in Christmas designs.

To produce your own, sprinkle 225 g (8 oz) blue household detergent into 1 litre (1¾ pints) boiling water. Add the leaves, stir them about with an old wooden spoon, and boil for 30 minutes.

Strain the leaves, rinse them under cold running water, then place them on sheets of newspaper. With an old toothbrush, brush off the green leaf tissue, working from the central vein out to the sides. Rinse the leaves again, dry them, then blot them between sheets of blotting paper. When they are completely dry, store them, interleaved with tissues, in a box.

Powder drying

If you would like to capture the romance of a token bunch of red roses, the loving thoughts that prompted a Mother's Day posy, or preserve the beauty of your favourite flowers almost forever, explore the exciting possibilities offered by 'powder drying'. In this process, you immerse flowers totally in a thoroughly dry agent (a desiccant, or drying powder) which extracts the moisture slowly from the petals, leaving the flowers crisp and brittle (and very delicate to handle) but otherwise virtually unchanged.

In the spring you can desiccant-dry hyacinths, lilac, polyanthus, primroses, wallflowers and even tiny violets and snowdrops, sprays of forsythia and apple, cherry and pear blossom. In summer the range widens considerably – buttercups and daisies, carnations and pinks, pansies and violas, marigolds, zinnias and other single and double composites, small side-shoots of delphinium and larkspur, slender stems of broom, long stems of London pride and stocks, small snippings of lily-of-the-valley and of sweet peas in all their multi-coloured glory; and rosebuds. Fully-opened roses may be worth a try, but the success rate is fairly low.

The bold and beautiful autumn chrysanthemums and dahlias powder-dry well. They need large amounts of desiccant, but fortunately, after use, it can be spread on baking trays, dried in a low oven and stored for re-use.

Even in winter there are treasures to seek out and dry. Sprays of brilliant yellow winter jasmine and other shrubs are especially good candidates.

You can use a wide range of household and other powders for drying flowers. Talcum powder, household borax, fine-ground silica gel crystals, fine corn-meal, fine oatmeal, and even well-washed and completely dry silver sand are all suitable. The first two, lightest in weight, are recommended for the most delicate of flowers.

The desiccant must be in close contact with every surface of every petal – any gaps let in the air, and therefore dampness, and therefore mould. Harvest the flowers when they are dry (it is an uphill, and thankless, task processing them otherwise) and discard any that are even slightly damaged.

Cut the plant material into short sprays – forsythia, broom, jasmine, larkspur, sweet pea, even hyacinth. As you have to fill every cavity of every flower with the powder, you need a fair bit of manual dexterity to cope with long stems or tiny hollows. Cut short the stems of individual flowers – be they buttercups or dahlias – to a length of only about 2.5 cm (1 inch). All these, and fleshy stems like hyacinth and bluebells, will need false stems.

Cover the base of a wooden or plastic box or an old biscuit-tin with a layer of just over 2.5 cm (1 inch) of the desiccant. Arrange flat or composite flowers on top so that they do not touch each other and sprinkle on the desiccant, letting it sift slowly through your fingers so that it covers each and every petal. Cup large trumpet-shaped flowers such as daffodils in one hand, fill the 'cups' with desiccant and then lower them gently on to the layer of powder. Lay short sprays of flowers on their sides, sprinkling the desiccant into any hollows, then cover them with the powder.

Cover the box, bind it with sticky-tape if necessary to make it airtight, and leave it undisturbed in a dry, warm, airy room.

Drying times vary according to the size and moisture content of the flowers. The range is from one day for violets and primroses, through two-to-three days for pinks, forsythia and zinnia, to five days and over for large dahlias.

To check whether the flowers are ready, scrape away the top layer of desiccant and touch the petals. They should crackle like cornflakes. If they feel the least bit soft or supple, cover them again and leave them for a day or two.

When the flowers are dry, gently remove them from the box, shake off any loose powder and brush them with a fine camel-hair brush to remove the last traces. Store the flowers between tissues in an airtight box.

Give the flowers false or reinforced stems according to type. Push a florist's wire through the fleshy stems of hyacinth and bluebell, and push a wire firmly into the calyx or flower centre of carnations, zinnias, marigolds. Bind the wire with florist's tape, or gutta percha. Short, dried stems that are firm can be pushed into the end of a hollow 'natural' stem – a piece of hollow wheat or grass for example. Once the flowers are wired or mounted on stems, store them upright, the stems pushed into dry foam, the heads separate and not touching.

You can arrange powder-dried flowers – carefully – with air-dried material; yellow rosebuds and winter jasmine with golden rod, deep red sweet peas with pink and white everlastings, perhaps. Or make a romantic nosegay of these precious papery-dry flowers for your dressing-table. Nothing could be prettier.

'Alternative' Christmas trees (see pages 82–3)

The fruit tree You will need: 1 22.5-cm (9-inch) clay flower-pot; 1 120-cm (4-foot) garden cane; holding material, such as heavy stones; peat, gravel or artificial 'snow' to cover top; a roll of binding wire; 2 metres (2 yards) 5-cm (2-inch)-mesh wire netting; short sprays of evergreens, such as cupressus, laurel, bay, ivy, juniper; rose hips, or spray-painted poppy seedheads; small clementines or satsumas and apples; florist's stub wires; Christmas tree clip-on birds; 5 metres (5 yards) 4-cm (1½-inch)-wide satin ribbon.

Secure the cane firmly in the pot, anchoring it with heavy stones. Cover the top with a layer of peat, gravel or artificial snow.

Wearing protective gardening gloves cut the netting into pieces about 30 cm (12 inches) long. Cut off the stiff edge, or selvage. Scrunch up the first piece of netting to form a small ball, cover it with the next, and the next, and so on, taking care to keep to the round shape. The finished ball will be about 35 cm (14 inches) in diameter.

Push the wire ball on to the cane and bind it with wire. Push the evergreens and the rose-hip stems through the gaps in the wire ball. You might have to secure the lower ones with a twist of wire.

Push a florist's stub wire through each piece of fruit and twist back the end to secure it. Twist the 'free' end into the wire ball. Clip the bird decorations on to branches. Double the ribbon, wrap it round the cane and tie it in a generous double bow.

The strawflower tree and the dried orange tree For each tree you will need: 1 22.5-cm (9-inch) clay flower pot; 1 120-cm (4-foot) garden cane; holding material and covering material as above; a roll of binding wire; 1 30-cm (12-inch) collapsible paper lampshade or wire frame; 18-cm (6-inch)-square thick paper; paper adhesive or sticky tape; 1 packet small double-sided adhesive strips; large dried strawflowers and other everlasting flowers or a collection of dried Chinese lanterns, honesty, statice, beech mast, chestnuts; Christmas bird decorations; 5 metres (5 yards) 4-cm (1½-inch)-wide satin ribbon.

Plant the cane as described for the fruit tree.

Open out the lampshade, insert the wire frame and lower it over the cane. Wire the frame firmly to the cane – an extra pair of hands is invaluable at this point. Stick the paper over the hole in the top of the shade.

Cut off the stems from the dried plant material. Cover the shades with the flowers, seedheads or nuts in your chosen colour combination. To do this, press the sticky strip first on to the shade, then press the flower on to it. Make sure there are no gaps.

Position a bird in flight. Finish off the tree with a trailing ribbon bow.

INDEX